Picture Books by

Latino Writers:

A Guide for Librarians,

Teachers, Parents

and Students

Sherry York

Linworth
PUBLISHING, INC.

Library of Congress Cataloging-in-Publication Data

York, Sherry, 1947-
    Picture Books by Latino Writers : a guide for librarians, teachers, parents, and students
by Sherry York.
      p. cm.
    Includes bibliographical references and index.
    ISBN 1-58683-052-X
    1.   Picture books for children--United States--Bio-bibliography. 2. American
Literature--Hispanic American authors--Bio-bibliography. 3. Children's literature,
American--Bio-bibliography. 4. Young adult literature, American--Bio-bibliography. 5.
Hispanic American authors--Biography. 6. Hispanic Americans in
Literature--Bibliography. 7. Hispanic American children--Books and
Reading--Bibliography. 8. Hispanic American teenagers--Books and
Reading--Bibliography. I. Title.

Z1037 .Y66 2002
810.8'09282—dc21

2001058182

Published by Linworth Publishing, Inc.
480 East Wilson Bridge Road, Suite L
Worthington, Ohio 43085

ISBN 1-58683-052-X

5 4 3 2 1

Table of Contents

Introduction

When my husband, an elementary school librarian, presented me with a book fair copy of *Chato's Kitchen*, it was love at first sight—with picture books by Latinos, that is! More than 20 years earlier, we had started our public school teaching careers in Crystal City, Texas, hometown of Tomás Rivera, son of migrant farm workers and a pioneer in Mexican-American literature, and of José Ángel Gutierrez, president of the school board and founder of the Raza Unida Party. It was there that I became aware of bilingual education and developed an interest in Latino literature.

As the years passed, I worked as a teacher, reading coordinator, and school librarian—always in places with significant numbers of Mexican-American students. As an educator, I tried to find materials that would be relevant to all my students. However, there were very few books at any level by Mexican Americans and none written for children or young adults.

Approximately 20 years later as a high school librarian, I began to see books by Gary Soto and Pat Mora. In the past decade, we have seen the publication of a few picture books, children's books, and young adult books by Latino authors. Only recently have there been enough Latino-authored books to fill a guide such as this one.

The most recent U.S. census indicates that the Latino population is increasing rapidly, and that Latinos are living, working, and reading across our country. The demand for Latino literature is increasing, especially for children. I wrote this guide to help you find Latino-authored picture books to meet your needs.

Purpose

The purpose of this guide is to assist teachers, librarians, parents, and students in selecting picture books to read, purchase, and use. This guide is offered

- to librarians with the hope that you will add diversity to your library collections by purchasing and promoting Latino literature to your clients;
- to teachers with the hope that you will incorporate Latino-authored picture books into your teaching;
- to parents and grandparents with the hope that you will read these books with your children, show them the value and joy of reading, and teach them to be proud of who they are and to be respectful of others; and
- to students of any age with the hope that you will learn about Latino literature and cultures.

Content

The guide is divided into seven sections. Part I discusses the need for authentic Latino literature. Part II provides publication and other relevant information about 65 picture books by Latinos. Part III includes biographical information about the authors, illustrators, and translators of these picture books. Part IV is a subject-title index. Part V lists literary awards these books have received and recommended reading lists on which they appear. Part VI provides information about the publishers and distributors of these and other Latino books and materials. Part VII is a bibliography of additional Latino-related picture books.

About the Author

Sherry York worked as an educator in Texas schools for 29 years before retiring. During her career, she taught English, language arts and reading, directed a Right to Read program, worked as a school librarian, completed an in-house automation of a library and served on two public library boards. She also conducted faculty in-service programs, served on district and regional committees, started and sponsored two student literary magazines and reviewed books for several magazines and journals. York and her husband Donnie, also a retired librarian, now reside in Ruidoso, New Mexico.

Selection Criteria

As I began compiling titles for this guide, I wanted to include as many picture books as possible, but limitations are always necessary. Picture books selected for this guide are

- written by Latino writers of the United States;
- original stories, not translations or folktales;
- set in the United States;
- in print and available for purchase; and
- in English or bilingual (Spanish-English) format.

In researching for this guide, I occasionally found negative comments about books in review sources. In many cases, I also found positive comments about the same books. Professional reviewers frequently disagree in their opinions because we all carry our individual backgrounds, perceptions, and prejudices to the reading experience. Although I have been a book reviewer for many years, I have chosen not to impose my critical viewpoint in this guide. Therefore, I have not included or rejected any picture book based on my opinions. I leave the evaluation of these books to each reader.

This guide is not meant to represent the "crème de la crème" but simply "what is." Latino writing by U.S. Latinos for children and young adults is emerging literature. There is not enough yet to be highly selective. I have provided available critical information. It is up to each reader to apply her or his own standards when deciding whether to read or purchase the books.

Because some of the picture books in this guide were written in English and translated into Spanish, the quality of translation may be a concern. Translation, like writing, is a complicated process. Skillful translators must do more than simply translate word by word. Anyone who has ever read the results of a computer translation will certainly appreciate this fact! The style and language of the original work must be considered. Complicating the situation is that there is no "universal Spanish" language. The Spanish spoken in northern New Mexico is different from that of southern Texas, and from Puerto Rican Spanish spoken on the island or in New York. Although Castilian or textbook Spanish may be proper, the translator must consider whether it accurately represents the way the characters in the story would actually speak.

For those readers who are concerned about the quality of translation, I have included references to the works of Dr. Isabel Schon, renowned author of many books that provide critical analyses of Spanish language and Latino heritage books. Her books and a related Web site are discussed in Part V. *Críticas*, a new quarterly guide from the *Library Journal* publications family, offers an English speaker's guide to Spanish language titles. In addition, some reviewers have commented about the quality of Spanish translation in reviews in other professional journals. As with the English versions, I urge readers to do the necessary research to determine whether a specific picture book will meet their individual needs.

I wrote this guide with the hope that readers will become informed and will make choices that will lead to greater use of picture books by Latino writers. Those readers who want more information may be interested in *Children's and Young Adult Literature by Latino Writers*, forthcoming from Linworth Publishing, Inc. As more picture books by Latinos are published, the number of titles may soon merit another picture book guide that examines folktales and fairy tales, myths and legends, holidays and celebrations, and more.

Part I

The Need for Authentic Latino Literature

To appreciate the need for this guide, the following facts require consideration:

- The dropout rate among Latino students is very high.
- Until fairly recently, few Latino writers were published.
- Latinos have been underrepresented in many of the libraries of the United States.
- Many excellent books by Latino authors remain undiscovered.
- The ethnicity of a book's author is relevant to its contents.

To understand the necessity of carefully selecting picture books by Latino writers, consider the following questions and answers:

1. What is the connection among family, culture, and picture books?
Many avid readers can recall a special picture book from childhood. Picture books are often associated with warm, cozy feelings of being read to by a loved one. In the past, before books became so readily available, grandparents or other elders were storytellers who painted word pictures by recounting stories about ancestors and events. In most modern cultures, storytelling elders are, sadly, no longer a part of families. Those purveyors of cultural history and pride are no more.

For many families, picture books have become a partial replacement for the family storytellers. Until recently, however, for Latino families, there were no culturally relevant picture books. Happily, that situation has changed. In the past 10 years, a number of Latino writers have published excellent picture books that deserve the attention of teachers, librarians, students, and parents.

2. Who are Latinos in the United States?
The term *Latino* arbitrarily groups peoples of Spanish-speaking ancestry in the United States. Numerous alternate terms are preferred by individuals and groups across the country. *Hispanic*

is the term used by the government to classify Mexican Americans, Mexicanos, Puerto Ricans, Puertoriqueños, Cubans, Dominicans, and immigrants from Spanish-speaking countries. Other terms preferred by various groups and individuals include *Latina, Latino, Hispano, Cubana, Cubano, Afro-Cuban, Nuyorican, Boricua, Chicano, Chicana, Mexican-American*, and others. Certainly in a country as culturally diverse as the United States, differing preferences are acceptable and should be respected. The term *Latino*, used in this book for the sake of convenience, is not gender specific and certainly does not exclude *Latinas* who are important in this field.

The single common feature shared by U.S. Latinos is that of a Spanish-speaking ancestry. Aside from the commonality of historical language, each group has a different history, each having followed a distinctly different path to become citizens of the United States.

Some Mexican-American families in the Southwest have been residents for generations; some predate the Pilgrims. Particularly in Texas, New Mexico, Arizona, California, and Colorado, many Mexican Americans trace their families back to colonial days before the Mexican War and the 1848 Treaty of Guadalupe Hidalgo, which transformed families from Mexican to American citizens. Other Mexican-American families have ancestors who came to the United States during the Mexican Revolution in the early decades of the twentieth century. Still others came as a part of the bracero program in which Mexican citizens came to the United States as workers to help alleviate the labor shortage during and after World War II.

Puerto Ricans from the island of Puerto Rico are citizens of the United States. Because Puerto Rico is a commonwealth, for generations Puerto Rican families have traveled to and from the mainland without the necessity of passports. Historically, Puerto Ricans on the mainland lived primarily along the eastern coast of the United States. Many Puerto Ricans have lived the "immigrant experience," although technically they are not immigrants.

Many Cuban Americans immigrated to the United States after Fidel Castro gained power in 1959. Others came as refugees in the 1980 Mariel boatlift. Many Cuban immigrants came first to Florida because of its proximity to Cuba. Motivated to flee Cuba because of the political situation, some older Cubans have lived their lives planning to return "someday" to the island. A majority of the earlier Cuban immigrants were from the middle and upper classes of society; they were educated and financially secure. Younger Cuban Americans born and raised in the United States have no memories of or yearnings for the homeland of their elders.

Another category of the Latino population consists of persons who have immigrated to the United States from Mexico, Central and South America, and the Caribbean Islands. What persons in this category share is not a common birth land, but common reasons for immigrating: to escape adverse economic or political situations that made life precarious or to take advantage of opportunities in the United States.

Latinos represent a heterogeneous group of peoples from many ethnic groups; they are from many backgrounds with divergent histories. Some Latinos speak only English, some are bilingual, and some are Spanish-speakers who have not yet learned the English language. It is also important to remember that Latinos are, first of all, human beings, not statistics and not political problems. All too often the human element is ignored in government, in education, and in societal interactions.

Readers wanting to learn more about Latino history and cultures are urged to refer to the *Handbook of Hispanic Cultures, Reference Library of Hispanic America, Harvest of Empire*, and *Hispanic American Almanac* listed in the "For Further Reading" list at the end of Part I.

3. Why is it important to know about Latinos in the United States?
According to the latest census, Latinos are the second-fastest growing population, and it is like-

ly that they will replace African Americans as the largest minority group of this country. The growth of the Hispanic population is taking place in states that have not traditionally had high percentages of Latino citizens. Much of the diffusion of Latinos into new areas is based on the pursuit of economic opportunities. California recently became the first minority-majority state. There are now more minority citizens in California than there are white or Anglo citizens. This trend is expected to continue (Booth).

To learn more about Latino demographic facts and figures, readers may consult the Tomás Rivera Policy Institute and the U.S. Census Web sites listed in "For Further Reading" at the end of Part I.

4. Why do teachers need to know about Latino literature?

Latino students have typically not done well in schools in the United States. Dropout rates among Latino students are high across much of the country. Many Latino leaders and writers attribute this situation to hostile school environments. Readers who would like to learn more about Latino dropout rates should consult the Intercultural Development Research Association and National Center for Educational Statistics Web sites listed in "For Further Reading" at the end of Part I.

Teachers across the country have become aware of the issues of accountability and curriculum standards in education. Several states require that students pass a standardized test to graduate from high school. Student achievement is a central focus of teaching, but students who are not present in the classroom will neither learn nor achieve. New Mexico author and professor Rudolfo Anaya has commented that some schools make Latino students feel that they don't belong and that their cultural values are not respected. In an article on <http://www.Latino.com>, Anaya called those students "push outs" (Hernandez).

Most students are intuitive and know immediately whether educators like and respect them. Teachers who are knowledgeable about the culture of Latino students are more likely to provide a welcoming, stress-free environment for Latino students of any age. Teachers familiar with curriculum standards for reading and writing should be able to easily integrate Latino literature into meaningful classroom activities. Learning and teaching about Latino cultures through Latino literature can be productive and enjoyable.

5. What should educators know about the Spanish language?

In the past, Latino students were often punished for speaking Spanish. More than a few prominent Latino writers, teachers, and professionals can recall being physically punished for speaking Spanish. Accounts by Latino writers tell of the hurt and shock they endured after being "caught" speaking their home language, even at recess on the playground. Such abuse and embarrassment in schools has left a legacy of mistrust and hatred that continues today. Readers interested in reading more about this aspect of Latino educational history should consult the nonfiction works of Anzaldua, Baca, Burciaga, Hart, Lomas Garza, Lopez-Stafford, Morales, Richard Rodriguez, and Villaseñor listed in "For Further Reading" at the end of Part I.

Many Latino parents concerned with assimilating into mainstream society have not taught their children Spanish. The majority of Latino students in the United States speak English. Some have retained the Spanish language and are bilingual. Yet others are monolingual, speaking only English.

Students who enter school speaking no English are likely to be recent immigrants. Because of a shifting population, schools that have not previously needed English-instruction programs may now need those programs. Teachers with no training or experience in language proficiency may find themselves working with students with a limited knowledge of English (Vazquez).

Spanish-speaking students are simply children or young adults who speak Spanish rather than English. Their native language has nothing to do with their intelligence or their humanity; they have not chosen to speak Spanish to be defiant or to cause problems in the classroom. Almost all students recognize the necessity of learning English and will respond positively in a supportive environment. Bilingual picture books are excellent tools for encouraging monolingual and bilingual students (and adults) to learn language in context rather than merely memorizing words in isolation.

6. How can teachers use picture books by Latino authors?

Teachers who are willing to support and encourage diversity in the classroom will find many uses for picture books by Latino writers. Having these books in a classroom will send the positive message that the teachers and school welcome Latinos. For non-Latino students, the books will send the message that all cultures are valued and respected in that environment.

Teachers of elementary-age children can use picture books by Latino writers just as they use other picture books. Uses may include reading centers, supplementary readers, classroom libraries, storytime, and curriculum support. Activities might include puppet shows, class plays, and special holiday events.

Teachers of middle and high school students can also find many uses for picture books. Teachers of English, Spanish, reading, and any subjects that lend themselves to classroom libraries or reading centers should consider including picture books in those libraries or centers.

Various activities in English and Spanish classes are applicable to picture books. Such activities might include grammatical or short story analyses, creative writing, oral reading, or more complex critical thinking exercises or projects. Teachers of Spanish might use bilingual picture books for translation exercises and to illustrate sentence structure, punctuation, verb tenses, and grammatical usage. Research and projects based on the lives and careers of the authors, illustrators, and translators included in this guide could be informative as well as relevant. Biographical or career research projects might involve students using library reference books and the Internet to learn about the lives and careers of picture book illustrators. Some writers and artists have Web sites and e-mail addresses so students might communicate with them either directly or through the publishers.

Certainly picture books can be useful in other subject areas. Picture books are a form of art and can be used for art-related lessons, such as analyzing artistic medium, style, and techniques. Teachers might use picture books as the basis for creative projects in which students design and illustrate picture books. Selected picture books can be used for oral reading assignments in speech classes. Parenting is often taught in child development classes or in home and family living classes. Reading to babies and children is an essential part of good parenting. Picture books should be available for oral reading projects in which students read to younger children in or out of the school environment.

This guide includes picture books on a multitude of subjects, including families, holidays, celebrations, animals, foods, libraries, homes, weaving, quilts, traditions, ghosts and spirits, religious celebrations, migrant workers, geography, careers, gangs, adoption, seasons, legends, and many more. Most of these topics relate directly or indirectly to geography, government, economics, history, and home economics. With a bit of creative thinking, teachers in many subject areas will find uses for picture books to enliven their teaching and to contribute to a welcoming school environment that values all cultures.

The ideas listed here are ones that I have generated. For more possible uses for picture books, readers should consult resources listed in "For Further Reading" at the end of Part I.

7.   How can librarians use picture books by Latino authors?
School librarians are charged with encouraging reading, supporting the curriculum, teaching and supporting the research process, and encouraging higher-level, critical thinking. In all of these areas of responsibility, school librarians deal with students, teachers, administrators, and frequently parents.

As the ethnic and linguistic diversity of student populations increases, the responsible school librarian who wishes to encourage reading must consider the ethnic background of the students she or he seeks to entice into the library and the world of reading. The culturally aware librarian will provide quality literature at various reading levels by writers representing the ethnic backgrounds of all students.

Only within the past 30 years have many works of literature by Latino writers been available in the United States. Latino writers still struggle to get their works into print, and the number of children's and young adult books by Latinos is still small, but the bottom line for publishers is sales. For that reason, it is vitally important that librarians work diligently to purchase books by minority authors and make them available in libraries.

The advent of computer technology has resulted in the presence in many schools of computerized testing programs, such as *Accelerated Reader* from Renaissance Learning and *Reading Counts* from Scholastic. Some titles in this guide have computer tests available. Other titles do not have tests, but both companies will consider suggestions of titles for new tests. By selecting, recommending, and suggesting picture books by Latino authors, librarians and teachers can make their voices heard and help create greater diversity in the literature tested by these commercial programs.

Picture books have been successfully incorporated into school library collections at all levels from kindergarten through high school. More and more picture books are being written for older audiences. Several award-winning picture books of recent years exhibit subject matter that will appeal to middle school and older students.

In addition, students (especially older ones) with dyslexia who deal continually with a nightmare of print in the school environment may find picture books with colorful pictures and fewer words per page more comfortable reading. Graphic novels, a relative of picture books, are becoming more commonplace in libraries. If picture books are used and enjoyed by their fellow students and teachers, students with reading disabilities will also embrace picture books without embarrassment.

Having picture books in the middle and high school library collection can meet a variety of reader needs, even those of the staff. School librarians at these levels should consider using picture books to educate teachers and administrators about Latino cultures. Including high-quality, culturally relevant books in the library will encourage readers of all ages to respect diversity. Thus the school environment becomes welcoming and inclusive to learners of all ethnic groups.

Just as school librarians are charged with encouraging reading and meeting the needs of an increasingly culturally diverse population, so also are librarians in public libraries faced with the same challenges. Depending on the size of their library, public librarians may work with everyone age one to 90 or with a specific age group. Regardless of the level or area of responsibility, the primary concern of public librarians is meeting the needs of their clients. Many public libraries would benefit from the purchase of picture books by Latino writers. By considering, selecting, and recommending books by Latinos, public librarians are contributing to more culturally relevant libraries and programs for Latinos and more diverse libraries for all users.

8. How can parents use picture books by Latino authors?

The greatest gifts that loving parents can give their children are a love for reading and an appreciation for their special family and cultural heritage. Family is an important element in the picture books in this guide, which includes a variety of Latino families from across the United States.

Choosing books for children can be a time-consuming and confusing process. It is hoped that this guide will assist parents in selecting quality books to share with their children. For parents who wish to teach their children English or Spanish through literature, this guide provides quality picture books that entertain as well as teach.

This guide describes and lists many picture books that illustrate the richness and beauty of Latino cultures in the United States today. The titles are presented for consideration by Latino parents who wish to pass on their cultural heritage. It is also for all parents who wish to help their children develop a respect for all cultures and a love of stories and literature.

9. How can students learn more about Latino literature?

Students of any age who wish to learn more about Latino literature have two basic options: enrolling in a formal class or developing an individual research and reading plan. Individual circumstances will determine the feasibility of these options.

Since the early 1970s, colleges and universities around the United States have begun to offer classes in Chicano literature, Mexican-American writers, Latinas and literature, and other multicultural courses that include Latino writers. Although Latino literature in general is receiving greater notice, the focus of college or university classes is not usually on children's or young adult literature. However, this option is worth considering if there is a college or university in the vicinity and the potential student of Latino literature has available time and funds.

A second option, developing an individual research and reading plan, allows a considerable amount of flexibility. Libraries can be invaluable for persons undertaking an individual plan of action. Borrowing privileges are usually available at public libraries by simply filling out a library card. Many large public libraries have branch libraries and bookmobiles for added convenience. If a public library is nearby, students should take advantage of its resources and the expertise of its librarians.

Students of Latino literature who have access to school or college libraries should utilize them. If resources in these libraries are lacking, students should inform the library personnel of their interest in Latino materials. This is important because most libraries have budget considerations and must carefully choose which books to order. A list of specific suggested titles, such as those presented in this guide, will be helpful and might be more effective than a general statement.

Depending on the individual's approach, reference books may be helpful. The student of Latino literature may wish to read about the lives of famous Latino writers and what they wrote. Usually, reference books are not checked out but are kept in the library so they will always be available.

In many libraries, some form of computerized catalog of books is available. After a bit of trial and error and practice, most online catalogs are not difficult to use, and most librarians will provide guidance and suggestions if needed. Computers have made it easier to efficiently locate library books.

For students who have access to the Internet, numerous Internet resources are available. Many library databases are searchable via the Internet so that library collections can be searched from outside the library. The Library of Congress is available on the Internet as a read-only resource in which book titles and records are available, but not the actual books.

The Web sites of several book companies, such as Amazon.com and Barnes & Noble, are excellent sources of information about books. From these Web pages, a user can determine the format (paperback, hardback, audio book, and so forth), the publisher, the number of pages, and whether the book is still in print. Many titles also contain a scan of the book cover, a summary, and reviews from periodicals and from customers who have read that book.

Students who are also parents may wish to combine the two roles so that parents and children read and learn together. As students of Latino literature become better informed, they will become aware of all sorts of opportunities to learn more. Some bookstores feature author's readings and book signings. Book festivals in various locales have become popular, with many authors doing readings and presentations. Once the student of Latino literature begins exploring, there are no limits. Reading one book leads to another and to another. Picture books are an excellent starting place.

10. Why is it important that these picture books be written by Latino authors?

Harriet Rohmer, founder of Children's Book Press, believes that everyone needs to "see themselves" in literature (Lazo). Adult Latinos frequently mention that they never read the works of Latino authors as children. When they discover Latino authors, their reaction is often a mixture of pride and excitement at seeing their culture reflected in a work of literature, and a feeling of anger that they reached adulthood without knowing that books by Latinos existed. In *Always Running*, Luis J. Rodríguez tells of his excitement as a teenager in finding a book about his own culture and his subsequent disappointment when an English teacher disregarded his newly discovered book and chastised him for not bringing in the assigned book (76).

In an article from *Instructor*, featured on the Scholastic Web site, author Gary Soto, one of the first Latino authors to publish books for children and young adults, recommends that the ethnicity of the author be considered when selecting multicultural literature. He believes that writers from other cultures lack the necessary experience and awareness that comes from living within the culture to write authentically about Latinos.

For too many years, too many Latinos have cut short their educational experience because they felt unwelcome in the public schools. Too many Latinos have grown up without having read a single work of literature by a Latino author. Too many library collections still do not adequately represent minority writers. Too many Latino students have completed their educational careers without reading anything related to their culture. We cannot erase the past, but we have the ability to work in the present to influence the future. We **can** change the world, one book at a time and one reader at a time.

Works Cited

Articles:

Booth, William. "California's Ethnic Diversity Grows." *Washington Post* 30 Mar. 2001: A03.

Hernandez, Macarena. "Author Rudolfo Anaya Promoting Curriculum Diversity." *Latino.com* 22 Sept. 2000. 25 Sept. 2000. <http://www.Latino.com>.

Lazo, Dorina K. "Multiculturalism Isn't New to Children's Literature But It's Gaining Ground." *The Fresno Bee* 16 Nov. 1999. Dec. 2000. <http://www.Latino.com>.

Vazquez, Ricardo. "Census 200: Latinos Moving Beyond Traditional Urban Enclaves." *Latino.com* 1 Sept. 2000. Sept. 2000. <http://www.Latino.com>.

Books:

Rodríguez, Luis J. *Always Running: La Vida Loca.* Curbstone Press, 1993.

For Further Reading

This bibliography is included for those wishing to learn more about picture books in education, the need for Latino literature, and U.S. Latino history and cultures.

Articles:

Johnson, Keith. "Children's Books in a High School Library? A Risky Question Worth Asking." *The Book Report* March/April 2001: 6-8.

Manifold, Marjorie Cohee. "Picture Books as a Social Studies Resource in the Elementary Classroom." *ERIC* #412168 March 1997: n.pag.

Books:

Alire, Camila, and Orlando Archibeque. *Serving Latino Communities: A How-to-do-it Manual For Librarians.* Neal-Schuman, 1998.

Anzaldúa, Gloria. *Borderlands: La Frontera.* Spinsters/Aunt Lute, 1987.

Baca, Jimmy Santiago. *Working in the Dark.* Red Crane Books, 1992.

Burciaga, José Antonio. *Spilling the Beans.* Joshua Odell Editions, 1995.

Forte, Imogene, and Sandra Schurr. *Using Favorite Picture Books to Stimulate Discussion and Encourage Critical Thinking.* Incentive Publications, 1995.

Gonzalez, Juan. *Harvest of Empire: A History of Latinos in America.* Viking, 2000.

Güereña, Salvador, ed. *Library Services to Latinos: An Anthology*. McFarland, 2000.

Hall, Susan. *Using Picture Storybooks to Teach Character Education*. Oryx Press, 2000.

Harms, Jeanne McLain, and Lucille Lettow. *Picture Books to Enhance the Curriculum*. H. W. Wilson, 1996.

Hart, Elva Treviño. *Barefoot Heart*. Bilingual Press/Editorial Bilingüe, 1999.

Hurst, Carol Otis, et al. *Curriculum Connections: Picture Books in Grades 3 and Up*. Linworth Publishing, 1998.

Immroth, Barbara, and Kathleen de la Peña McCook, eds. *Library Services to Youth of Hispanic Heritage*. McFarland, 2000.

Kanellos, Nicolás, ed. *Reference Library of Hispanic America*. 3 vols. Gale Research, 1993.

Kiefer, Barbara Z. *The Potential of Picturebooks: From Visual Literacy to Aesthetic Understanding*. Merrill, 1995.

Lomas Garza, Carmen. *A Piece of My Heart/Pedacito de mi Corazón*. The New Press, 1991.

Lomelí, Francisco, ed. *Handbook of Hispanic Cultures in the United States: Literature and Art*. Arte Público Press, 1993.

Lopez-Stafford, Gloria. *A Place in El Paso*. University of New Mexico Press, 1996.

Merchant, Guy, Huw Thomas, and Kath Cooper, eds. *Picture Books for the Literacy Hour: Activities for Primary Teachers*. David Fulton, 1999.

Moller, Sharon Chickering. *Library Service to Spanish Speaking Patrons: A Practical Guide*. Libraries Unlimited, 2000.

Morales, Dionicio. *Dionicio Morales: A Life in Two Cultures*. Piñata Books, 1997.

Rodriguez, Richard. *Days of Obligation*. Viking, 1992.

Ryan, Bryan, and Nicolás Kanellos, eds. *Hispanic American Almanac*. U·X·L, 1995.

Saunders, Sheryl Lee. *Look—and Learn!: Using Picture Books in Grades Five Through Eight*. Heinemann, 1999.

Spitz, Ellen Handler. *Inside Picture Books*. Yale University Press, 1999.

Tiedt, Iris McClellan. *Teaching with Picture Books in the Middle School*. International Reading Association, 2000.

Villaseñor, Victor. *Walking Stars*. Arte Público Press, 1994.

Zimmerman, Marc. *U.S. Latino Literature: An Essay and Annotated Bibliography*. MARCH/Abrazo Press, 1992.

Web sites:

"Dropout Stats. Education Statistics. IDRA Research Result." *Intercultural Development Research Association*. <http://www.idra.org/Research/edstats.htm#dropouts>.

"How to Choose the Best Multicultural Books." *Instructor*. <http://teacher.scholastic.com/lessonrepro/lessonplans/instructor/multicultural.htm>.

"No More Excuses: Final Report of the Hispanic Dropout Project." *National Center for Education Statistics*. <http://www.ncbe.gwu.edu/miscpubs/hdp/final.htm#background>.

Tomás Rivera Policy Institute. <http://www.trpi.org>.

U.S. Census Bureau. <http://www.census.gov/prod/www/titles.html>.

Part II

The Picture Books

This section contains descriptions of many outstanding picture books by Latino writers. Information is included so that readers may make reading or purchase lists. Few readers have the time and money to read or purchase every title listed, so related information is included to help readers select the best book(s) to suit their purposes.

For each title, the **author, illustrator**, and **translator** are listed. Part III provides additional information on these persons. The **language** of each book is listed also. The book format may be one book in English, one bilingual book, or two books—one in English and one in Spanish. The **description** includes the number of pages, type of illustrations, and the size in centimeters.

Information in the **published** category includes the company or companies that have published that title. Library of Congress numbers (LC#) are provided. All **editions** and specific International Standard Book numbers (ISBNs) are listed. Editions may be paperbacks (pb.), hardcover (hc.), or library binding (lib. bdg.). For each title a **summary** is provided. Book summaries were taken from Library of Congress records except in cases where no Library of Congress record existed. The **subjects** listed also came from the Library of Congress. A subject-title index is included in Part IV.

If computer tests are available through the *Accelerated Reader* program from Renaissance Learning or the *Reading Counts* program from Scholastic, that information is listed. The tests may be listed as **English Tests** or **Spanish Tests**. These commercial programs are frequently used in a school setting, and titles are frequently added. Because the programs are available for purchase in separate components, the tests that each school owns will vary. Both companies have Web sites and solicit title recommendations, so new tests may become available.

If a book has been **reviewed** in a major review journal, those journals are listed for those wishing to read more about a title. Because the review process is ongoing, reviews other than those listed may be published as this guide goes to press, or they may be forthcoming. Most reviews in local or regional newspapers and magazines have not been included.

Information about books that have received or been nominated for major **awards** is provided. For more information about awards, see Part V. Some states and organizations provide **lists** of recommended book titles. Other states sponsor an annual reading list from which students may read and vote for favorites, which then receive an award. This is an ongoing process, so the lists section will change with time. Explanations of some lists are provided in Part V.

Also included in the **lists** are references to Dr. Isabel Schon's books that contain evaluations of many Spanish-language and Latino heritage books. Those readers concerned about the quality of translations are urged to consult Dr. Schon's books. More information about her lists and evaluations is provided in Part V.

Internet **Web sites** that offer lesson plans or activities for students, teachers, librarians, or parents, and that focus primarily on a specific book are included in this section. Certainly this listing is not all-inclusive. Web sites frequently disappear or change addresses, and new sites are added daily. These listings reflect those sites that seem useful at this time.

Abuela

Author: Arthur Dorros

Illustrator: Elisa Kleven

Translator: Sandra Marulanda Dorros

Language: One book in English and one book in Spanish

Description: 40 pages, color illustrations, 28 cm

Published:
New York: Dutton Children's Books, 1991 [English]
New York: Dutton Children's Books, 1995 [Spanish]

LC # 90021459 [English]
95012202 [Spanish]

English Editions:
Dutton 0525447504 lib. bdg.
Puffin 0140562257 pb.
Econo-Clad 0613028023 hc.

Spanish Editions:
Dutton 0525454381 hc.
Puffin 0140562265 pb.
Econo-Clad 0613028368 hc.

Summary: While riding on a bus with her grandmother, a little girl imagines that they are carried up into the sky and fly over the sights of New York City.

Subjects:
Flight—Fiction
Grandmothers—Fiction
Hispanic Americans—Fiction
Imagination—Fiction
New York (N. Y.)—Fiction
Spanish language materials
[Spanish version]

English Tests:
Accelerated Reader *Young Adventures*
Reading Counts *Hispanic Experience for K–2, Our Grandparents, Literacy Place 2000*
Grade K Read Alouds

Spanish Tests:
Accelerated Reader *¡Viva Español!*

Reviewed: *Booklist, Horn Book, Kirkus, New York Times, Publishers Weekly, School Library Journal*

Lists: ALA Notable Books, California Department of Education Recommended Literature List, New York Public Library 100 Picture Books Everyone Should Know, Notable Social Studies Books, Parent's Choice, Schon's *Best of the Latino Heritage, 1997*

Web sites:
[teachers]
<http://www.sdcoe.k12.ca.us/score/abuela/abuelatg.html>
[students]
<http://www.crpc.rice.edu/CRPC/Women/GirlTECH/Participants/jpeckham/Lessons/Family/abuela.html>

Notes:
1. This book was a Reading Rainbow selection in 1993.
2. Art is mixed-media collage with ink, pastels, watercolor, and cut paper.
3. A glossary and pronunciation guide for Spanish words and phrases is included.

Abuelita's Paradise
El Paraíso de Abuelita

Author: Carmen Santiago Nodar

Illustrator: Diane Paterson

Translator: Teresa Mlawer

Language: One book in English and one book in Spanish

Description: 32 pages, color illustrations, 21 cm

Published: Morton Grove, Ill.: Albert Whitman, 1992

LC# 91042330 [English]
 92003767 [Spanish]

English Edition:
 Whitman 0807501298 lib. bdg.

Spanish Edition:
 Whitman 0807563463 lib. bdg.

Summary: Although her grandmother has died, Marita sits in Abuelita's rocking chair and remembers the stories Abuelita told of life in Puerto Rico.

Subjects:
 Death—Fiction
 Grandmothers—Fiction
 Puerto Rico—Fiction
 Spanish language materials [Spanish version]

English Tests:
 Accelerated Reader *Concept Books (Albert Whitman)*
 Reading Counts Individual Quiz

Spanish Test:
 Accelerated Reader *¡Viva Español!*

Reviewed: *Booklist, Horn Book, Kirkus, Publishers Weekly, School Library Journal*

Web site: [students]
 <http://www.si.edu/scmre/our_story.html>

Note: A videocassette, *Abuelita's Paradise*, produced by Society for Visual Education in 1992, is available.

The Adventures of Connie and Diego
Las aventuras de Connie y Diego

Author: Maria Garcia

Illustrator: Malaquias Montoya

Translator: Alma Flor Ada

Language: One bilingual book

Description: 24 pages, color illustrations, 25 cm [revised edition]

Published: San Francisco: Children's Book Press/Libros para niños, 1978.
 rev. edition, 1987

LC# 86017132

Editions:
Children's 089239028X lib. bdg.
Children's 0892391243 pb.
Children's 0892390514 audiotape cassette
Children's 0892390336 book and cassette
Econo-Clad 0785735968 hc.

Series: *Fifth World Tales(Cuentos del quinto mundo)*

Summary: Tired of being laughed at because they are different, a pair of multicolored twins decide to run away and find a new place to live.

Subjects:
Brothers and sisters—Fiction
Prejudices—Fiction
Spanish language—Readers
Spanish language materials—Bilingual
Twins—Fiction

Spanish Test:
Accelerated Reader *¡Viva Español!*

Reviewed: *Booklist, Horn Book, Interracial Books for Children Bulletin, Los Angeles Times*

Web site: [teachers]
<http://www.ladb.unm.edu/retanet/plans/soc/kent.html>

Notes:
1. With a copyright date of 1978, this is one of the earliest bilingual picture books with an original story by a Latino writer in the United States.
2. Page 24 contains "The Author Talks About Her Story."

América Is Her Name
La llaman América

Author: Luis J. Rodríguez

Illustrator: Carlos Vázquez

Translator: Tino Villanueva

Language: One book in English and one book in Spanish

Description: 32 pages, color illustrations, 26 cm

Published: Willimantic, CT: Curbstone Press, 1996 [English and Spanish versions]

LC# 96021345 [English]
     96024508 [Spanish]

English Editions:
Curbstone 1880684403 hc.
Econo-Clad 0613072316 hc.

Spanish Edition:
Curbstone 1880684411 hc.

Summary: A Mixteca Indian from Oaxaca, América Soliz, suffers from the poverty and hopelessness of her Chicago ghetto, made more endurable by her desire and determination to be a poet.

Subjects:
Mexican Americans—Fiction
Mexican Americans—Juvenile fiction
Poets—Fiction

Spanish language materials
[Spanish version]

English Test:
  Accelerated Reader Individual Quiz

Reviewed: *Horn Book, Publishers Weekly, School Library Journal*

Awards: Patterson Prize, Skipping Stones Award

Angels Ride Bikes and Other Fall Poems
Los Ángeles Andan en Bicicleta y otros poemas de otoño

Author: Francisco X. Alarcón

Illustrator: Maya Christina Gonzalez

Language: One bilingual book

Description: 32 pages, color illustrations, 28 cm

Published: San Francisco: Children's Book Press/Libros para niños, 1999

LC# 99010193

Edition:
  Children's 089239160X hc.

Summary: In this bilingual collection of poems, the renowned Mexican-American poet revisits and celebrates his childhood memories of fall in the city and growing up in Los Angeles.

Subjects:
  American poetry
  Autumn—Juvenile poetry
  Children's poetry, American
  Children's poetry, American—
    Translations into Spanish.
  Children's poetry, Hispanic American
    (Spanish)—Translations into English
  Family—California—Los Angeles—
    Juvenile poetry
  Los Angeles (Calif.)—Juvenile poetry
  Los Angeles (Calif.)—Poetry
  Mexican American families—California—
    Los Angeles—Juvenile poetry
  Mexican Americans—Poetry
  Spanish language materials—Bilingual

Reviewed: *Booklist, Horn Book, Kirkus, Publishers Weekly, School Library Journal*

Awards: Américas, Tomás Rivera

List: Parents' Choice

Barrio: José's Neighborhood
Barrio: El barrio de José

Author and illustrator: George Ancona

Language: One book in English and one book in Spanish

Description: 48 pages, color illustrations, 24 × 26 cm

Published: San Diego: Harcourt Brace, 1998

LC#   97029667 [English]
     97042307 [Spanish]

English Editions:
    Harcourt 0152010491 lib. bdg.
    Harcourt 0152010483 pb.
    Econo-Clad 061311308X lib. bdg.

Spanish Editions:
    Harcourt 0152018085 pb.
    Econo-Clad 0613113098 lib. bdg.

Summary: This book presents life in a barrio in San Francisco, describing the school, recreation, holidays, and family life of an eight-year-old boy who lives there.

Subjects:
    Mexican American families—California—San Francisco—Social life and customs—Juvenile literature
    Mexican Americans—San Francisco (Calif.)
    Mission District (San Francisco, Calif.)—Social life and customs—Juvenile literature
    San Francisco (Calif.)—Social life and customs
    San Francisco (Calif.)—Social life and customs—Juvenile literature
    Spanish language materials [Spanish version]

English Tests:
    Accelerated Reader Individual Quiz
    Reading Counts Individual Quiz

Spanish Test:
    Accelerated Reader *¡Viva Español!*

Reviewed: *Booklist, Horn Book, Multicultural Review, School Library Journal*

Awards: Américas, Pura Belpré

Lists: Notable Social Studies Books for Young People, Schon's *Best of the Latino Heritage,* 1997

Note: A glossary of Spanish words is included.

Benito's Bizcochitos
Los bizcochitos de Benito

Author: Ana Baca

Illustrator: Anthony Accardo

Translator: Julia Mercedes Castilla

Language: One bilingual book

Description: 32 pages, color illustrations, 29 cm

Published: Houston, TX: Piñata Books, 1999

LC# 99024809

Editions:
    Arte Público 1558852646 hc.
    Arte Público 1558852654 pb.

Summary: As Christine and her grandmother prepare to make the traditional Christmas cookies known as bizcochitos, the grandmother tells the story of how a magical butterfly first introduced these sweet treats to her great-grandfather, a shepherd in the hills of New Mexico.

Subjects:
    Christmas—Fiction
    Cookies—Fiction

    Mexican Americans—Juvenile fiction
    Mexican Americans—Fiction
    Spanish language materials—Bilingual

English Test:
    Accelerated Reader *Legends and Lore*

Spanish Test:
    Accelerated Reader *¡Viva Español!*

Reviewed: *Horn Book, School Library Journal*

Award: Tomás Rivera

Note: A recipe for bizcochitos in Spanish and in English is included.

Big Bushy Mustache

Author: Gary Soto

Illustrator: Joe Cepeda

Language: One book in English

Description: 32 pages, color illustrations, 29 cm

Published: New York: Knopf, 1998

LC# 97018211

Editions:
    Knopf 067998030X lib. bdg.
    Knopf 0679880305 hc.

Summary: To look more like his father, Ricky borrows a mustache from a school costume, but when he loses it on the way home, his father comes up with a replacement.

Subjects:
    Fathers and sons—Fiction
    Mexican Americans—Fiction
    Mustaches—Fiction

English Tests:
    Accelerated Reader *Tree House Favorites*
    Reading Counts Individual Quiz

Reviewed: *Booklist, Horn Book, School Library Journal*

Award: Américas

Lists: Missouri Show Me Readers List 1999–2000 and 2000–2001

Note: Ricky's mustache is a prop for the class play for Cinco de Mayo.

Big Enough
Bastante grande

Author: Ofelia Dumas Lachtman

Illustrator: Enrique O. Sánchez

Translator: Yanitzia Canetti

Language: One bilingual book

Description: 32 pages, color illustrations, 28 cm

Published: Houston, TX: Piñata Books, 1998

LC#   97026672

Editions:
Arte Público 1558852212 hc.
Arte Público 1558852395 pb.

Summary: When a treasured piñata is stolen, little Lupita discovers that she is big enough to help her mother get it back.

Subjects:
Mexican Americans—Fiction
Mothers and daughters—Fiction
Piñatas—Fiction
Size—Fiction
Spanish language materials—Bilingual
Stealing—Fiction

Spanish Test:
Accelerated Reader *¡Viva Español!*

Reviewed: *Horn Book, School Library Journal*

Award: Tomás Rivera

A Birthday Basket for Tía
Una canasta de cumpleaños para Tía

Author: Pat Mora

Illustrator: Cecily Lang

Language: One book in English and one book in Spanish

Description: 32 pages, color illustrations, 21 cm

Published: New York: Macmillan, 1992 [English]; New York: Aladdin Paperbacks, 1997 [Spanish]

LC#   91015753 [English]
96033092 [Spanish]

English Editions:
Simon & Schuster 0027674002 lib. bdg.
Aladdin Paperbacks 0689813287 pb.
Econo-Clad 0613021533 hc.

Spanish Edition:
Aladdin 0689813252 pb.

Summary: With the help and interference of her cat, Chica, Cecilia prepares a surprise gift for her great-aunt's 90th birthday.

Subjects:
Birthdays—Fiction
Cats—Fiction

Gifts—Fiction
Great-aunts—Fiction
Mexican Americans—Fiction
Spanish language materials
    [Spanish version]

English Tests:
Accelerated Reader *Librarians Pick '97*
Reading Counts *Literacy Place*

Spanish Tests:
Accelerated Reader *¡Viva Español!*
Reading Counts *Nonfiction Collection for K–2, Showcase on Diversity K–2*

Reviewed: *Booklist, Horn Book, Kirkus, Publishers Weekly, School Library Journal*

Web sites: [teachers]
<http://www.mcps.k12.md.us/curriculum/
socialstd/MBD/Birthday_Basket.html>

The Birthday Swap
¡Qué sorpresa de cumpleaños!

Author and illustrator: Loretta Lopez

Language: One book in English and one book in Spanish

Description: 32 pages, color illustrations, 25 cm

Published: New York: Lee & Low Books, 1997

LC#   96024136 [English]
       97006668 [Spanish]

English Editions:
Lee & Low 1880000474 hc.
Lee & Low 188000089X pb.

Spanish Editions:
Lee & Low 1880000555 hc.
Lee & Low 1880000563 pb.
Econo-Clad 0613057457 hc.

Summary: A five-year-old Mexican-American girl who will not be six until December has a great deal to celebrate when her sister swaps birthdays with her in the summer.

Subjects:
Birthdays—Fiction
Mexican Americans—Fiction
Sisters—Fiction
Spanish language materials [Spanish version]

English Tests:
Accelerated Reader *Edison AR 2001 Disk 7, Folktales & Freedom, Multicultural Library (Lee & Low)*
Reading Counts *Hispanic Experience for K–2; Multicultural Titles for Grades 3–5*

Spanish Test:
Reading Counts *Solares Library 1*

Reviewed: *Booklist, Bulletin of the Center for Children's Books, Horn Book, Midwest Book Review, Publishers Weekly, School Library Journal*

Award: Américas

Lists: Children's Choices, Schon's *Recommended Books in Spanish, 1996–1999*

Notes:
1. A glossary of Spanish words is included at the beginning of the English version.
2. Illustrations are done in colored pencil and gouache.

Calling the Doves
El canto de las palomas

Author: Juan Felipe Herrera

Illustrator: Elly Simmons

Language: One bilingual book

Description: 30 pages, color illustrations, 26 cm

Published: San Francisco: Children's Book Press/Libros para niños, 1995

LC# 94045901

Edition:
Children's 0892391324 hc.

Summary: The author recalls his childhood in the mountains and valleys of California with his farmworker parents, who inspired him with poetry and song.

Subjects:
Agricultural workers—California—Juvenile literature
Authors, American
California—Social life and customs—Juvenile literature
Children of migrant laborers—California—Juvenile literature
Herrera, Juan Felipe
Herrera, Juan Felipe—Childhood and youth—Juvenile literature
Herrera, Juan Felipe—Homes and haunts—California—Juvenile literature
Mexican American families—California—Juvenile literature
Mexican Americans—Biography
Migrant labor—California
Spanish language materials—Bilingual

English Test:
Accelerated Reader Individual Quiz

Spanish Test:
Accelerated Reader *¡Viva Español!*

Reviewed: *Booklist, Bulletin of the Center for Children's Books, Horn Book, Multicultural Review, School Library Journal*

Awards: Américas, Ezra Jack Keats Award

Lists: California Department of Education Recommended Literature List, Children's Choices, *Smithsonian* Notable Books for Children, Teachers' Choices

Web site: [teachers]
<http://www.sfusd.k12.ca.us/schwww/sch634/FHPY2K/Outlinelessons.html>

Note: *The Upside Down Boy* continues this story.

Calor: A Story of Warmth for All Ages

Author: Juanita Alba

Illustrator: Amado M. Peña, Jr.

Language: One bilingual book

Description: 31 pages, color illustrations, 26 × 28 cm

Published: Waco, TX: WRS Publications, 1995

LC# 94026332

Editions:
    Lectorum 1880507269 hc.
    WRS 1567960693 hc.

Summary: This book explains and illustrates the meaning of warmth in family and nature.

Subject: Family

Spanish Test:
    Accelerated Reader ¡*Viva Español!*

Reviewed: *Horn Book*

Award: Tomás Rivera

Illustrations include:
    Colcha Series: La Promesa (The Promise)
    La Centinela (The Sentinel)
    Los Cuentos (The Stories)
    Danza de Colores (Dance of Colors)
    Abuelita: La Cuentista (Grandmother: The Storyteller)
    Colcha Series: La Tejedora (The Weaver)
    Danza del Bisonte (Dance of the Bison)
    Patrónes (Patterns)
    Danza de los Artesanos (Dance of the Artisans)
    El Sábado, Día del Mercado (Saturday: Market Day)
    Haciendo Pan (Making Bread)
    Coming Home
    Los Regalos (The Gifts)
    Artesanas de Taos (Artisans of Taos)
    Autoretrato (Self Portrait)

Carlos and the Squash Plant
Carlos y la planta de calabaza

Author: Jan Romero Stevens

Illustrator: Jeanne Arnold

Translator: Patricia Hinton Davison

Language: One bilingual book

Description: 32 pages, color illustrations, 29 cm

Published: Flagstaff, AZ: Northland, 1993

LC#   92082137

Editions:
    Northland 0873585593 hc.
    Northland 0873586255 pb.

Summary: Having ignored his mother's warnings about what will happen if he doesn't bathe after working on his family's New Mexican farm, Carlos awakens one morning to find a squash growing out his ear.

Subjects:
    Cleanliness—Fiction
    Farm life—Fiction
    New Mexico—Fiction
    Spanish language materials
    Squashes—Fiction

English Tests:
    Accelerated Reader Individual Quiz
    Reading Counts *Multicultural Read Alouds K–2, Literacy Place*

Spanish Test:
    Accelerated Reader ¡*Viva Español!*

Reviewed: *Booknews, Horn Book, School Library Journal*

Note: A recipe for calabacitas (squash) is included.

Carlos and the Cornfield
Carlos y la milpa de maíz

Author: Jan Romero Stevens

Illustrator: Jeanne Arnold

Translator: Patricia Hinton Davison

Language: One bilingual book

Description: 32 pages, color illustrations, 29 cm

Published: Flagstaff, AZ: Northland, 1995

LC#   95002980

Editions:
Northland 0873585698 hc.
Northland 0873587359 pb.

Summary: When he sees the results of not following his father's instructions on the proper way to plant corn, a young boy tries to make things right.

Subjects:
Corn—Fiction
Farm life—New Mexico—Fiction
New Mexico—Fiction
Spanish language materials—Bilingual

English Test:
Reading Counts Individual Quiz

Spanish Test:
Accelerated Reader *¡Viva Español!*

Reviewed: *Booklist, School Library Journal*

Lists: New Mexico Land of Enchantment Booklist 1998–1999, Schon's *Recommended Books in Spanish, 1991–1995*

Web site: [teachers]
<http://www.unm.edu/~hmahn/lesson plans442.html>

Notes:
1. Illustrations were done with oil paints on gessoed watercolor paper.
2. A recipe for cornmeal pancakes in English and in Spanish is included.

Carlos and the Skunk
Carlos y el zorrillo

Author: Jan Romero Stevens

Illustrator: Jeanne Arnold

Translator: Patricia Hinton Davison

Language: One bilingual book

Description: 32 pages, color illustrations, 29 cm

Published: Flagstaff, AZ: Rising Moon, 1997

LC#   96043677

Edition:
Rising Moon 0873585917 hc.

Summary: When Carlos tries to show off for his friend Gloria by catching a skunk, he gets more than he bargained for.

Subjects:
    Farm life—New Mexico—Fiction
    New Mexico—Fiction
    Skunks—Fiction
    Spanish language materials—Bilingual

English Tests:
    Accelerated Reader Individual Quiz
    Reading Counts *Friendship Stories for*
    Intermediates

Spanish Test:
    Accelerated Reader *¡Viva Español!*
Reviewed: *Booklist, Horn Book*

Award: Américas

Notes:
1. Illustrations were made with oil paints on gessoed watercolor paper.
2. Recipes for fresh tomato salsa (salsa de tomate fresca) are included.

Carlos and the Carnival
Carlos y la feria

Author: Jan Romero Stevens

Illustrator: Jeanne Arnold

Language: One bilingual book

Description: 32 pages, color illustrations, 29 cm

Published: Flagstaff, AZ: Rising Moon, 1999

LC#   98047521

Edition:
    Rising Moon 0873587332 hc.

Summary: Carlos ignores his father's advice about being careful how he spends his money at the carnival, and soon his pockets are empty.

Subjects:
    Money—Fiction
    Spanish language materials—Bilingual

Reviewed: *Booklist, Horn Book, School Library Journal*

Notes:
1. Illustrations are oil paints on gessoed watercolor paper.
2. A recipe for sopaipillas in Spanish and in English is included.

Carlos Digs to China
Carlos excava hasta la China

Author: Jan Romero Stevens

Illustrator: Jeanne Arnold

Language: One bilingual book

Description: 32 pages, color illustrations, 29 cm

Published: Flagstaff, AZ: Rising Moon, 2001

LC#   00051009

Edition:
Rising Moon 0873587642 hc.

Summary: After a visit to a Chinese restaurant, Carlos decides to dig a hole to China so he can have egg rolls instead of rice and beans and tortillas.

Subjects:
Cookery, Chinese—Fiction
Holes—Fiction
Spanish language materials—Bilingual

Reviewed: *School Library Journal*

Notes:
1. This is the final Carlos book. Jan Romero Stevens died in 2000. A part of the proceeds from the sale of this book will be donated to the American Cancer Society's Tell-A-Friend project in Flagstaff, Arizona, a breast cancer early detection program.
2. Illustrations were done in acrylic paints on gessoed watercolor paper.
3. A recipe for sweet rice/arroz dulce is included.
4. The last page contains a tribute to Jan Romero Stevens.

Chato's Kitchen
Chato y su cena

Author: Gary Soto

Illustrator: Susan Guevara

Translator: Alma Flor Ada

Language: One book in English and one book in Spanish

Description: 32 pages, color illustrations, 28 cm

Published: New York: Putnam's, 1995

LC# 93043503

English Editions:
Putnam's 0399226583 lib. bdg.
Paper Star 0698116003 pb.
Econo-Clad 0613035895 lib bdg.

Spanish Editions:
Econo-Clad 0613047109 lib.bdg.
Paper Star 0698116011 pb.
Live Oak Media 0874994373 book + cassette

Summary: To get the "ratoncitos," little mice, who have moved into the barrio to come to his house, Chato the cat prepares all kinds of good food: fajitas, frijoles, salsa, enchiladas, and more.

Subjects:
Cats—Fiction
Los Angeles (Calif.)—Fiction
Mice—Fiction
Spanish language materials [Spanish version]

English Tests:
Accelerated Reader *Fables, Fantasies & Fun*; *Edison AR 2001, GA Book Award 97–98*
Reading Counts *Hispanic Experience for K–2*

Spanish Tests:
Accelerated Reader *¡Viva Español!*
Reading Counts *Pan America K–2*

Reviewed: *Booklist, Horn Book, Publishers Weekly, School Library Journal*

Awards: Américas, Pura Belpré, Tomás Rivera

Lists: ALA Notable Books, California Young Reader Medal Reading List, Parents' Choice, Scholastic's 200 For 2000, Schon's *Recommended Books in Spanish, 1996–1999*

Note: *Chato's Kitchen* is available as an animated 11-minute videocassette from Weston Woods. It is narrated by Cheech Marin with music by Jerry Dale McFadden.

Chato and the Party Animals

Author: Gary Soto

Illustrator: Susan Guevara

Language: One book in English

Description: 32 pages, color illustrations, 29 cm

Published: New York: Putnam, 2000

LC# 96037501

Edition:
Putnam 0399231595 lib. bdg.

Summary: Chato decides to throw a "pachanga" for his friend Novio Boy, who has never had a birthday party.

Subjects:
Birthdays—Fiction
Cats—Fiction
Los Angeles (Calif.)—Fiction
Parties—Fiction

English Tests:
Accelerated Reader *My Animal Friends, Vol. II*
Reading Counts *ALA Notables Younger/ Middle Readers 2001*

Reviewed: *Booklist, Kirkus, School Library Journal*

Award: Tomás Rivera

List: ALA Notable Books

Note: This book is the sequel to *Chato's Kitchen*.

Chave's Memories
Los recuerdos de Chave

Author: María Isabel Delgado

Illustrator: Yvonne Symank

Language: One bilingual book

Description: 32 pages, color illustrations, 29 cm

Published: Houston, TX: Piñata Books, 1996

LC# 95047732

Edition:
Arte Público 1558850848 hc.

Summary: A woman recalls childhood visits to her grandparents' ranch in Mexico, where she and her brother played with her cousins and listened to the stories of an old Indian ranch hand.

Subjects:
Mexico—Fiction

Play—Fiction
Spanish language materials—Bilingual
Storytelling—Fiction

Spanish Test:
Accelerated Reader *¡Viva Español!*

Reviewed: *School Library Journal*

Awards: Américas, Tomás Rivera

The Christmas Gift
El regalo de Navidad

Author: Francisco Jiménez

Illustrator: Claire B. Cotts

Language: One bilingual book

Description: 32 pages, color illustrations, 29 cm

Published: Boston: Houghton Mifflin, 2000

LC# 99026224

Edition:
Houghton 0395928699 hc.

Summary: His family has to move again a few days before Christmas in order to find work, and Panchito worries that he will not get the gift he has been wanting.

Subjects:
Christmas—Fiction
Mexican Americans—Fiction
Migrant labor—Fiction

Spanish language materials—Bilingual

English Tests:
Accelerated Reader Individual Quiz
Reading Counts *ALA Notables
Younger/Middle Readers 2001*

Spanish Test:
Accelerated Reader Individual Quiz

Reviewed: *Booklist, Horn Book*

Award: Tomás Rivera

List: ALA Notable Books

Notes:
1. Illustrations are acrylic paint on water-color paper.
2. An author's note on the last page of the book reveals that this story is based on experiences of his childhood in California.

The Christmas Tree
El árbol de Navidad
A Christmas Rhyme in English and Spanish

Author: Alma Flor Ada

Illustrator: Terry Ybáñez

Language: One bilingual book

Description: 32 pages, color illustrations, 27 cm

Published: New York: Hyperion Books for
Children, 1997

LC#   96038218

Editions:
Hyperion 078682123X lib. bdg.
Hyperion 0786801514 hc.

Summary: A cumulative rhyme describes the
decorating of the family Christmas tree.

Subjects:
Christmas—Fiction
Christmas trees—Fiction
Spanish language materials—Bilingual
Stories in rhyme

Notes:
1. In an author's note at the end of the
book, Alma Flor Ada writes about
Christmases of her childhood in Cuba;
Christmas traditions such as posadas,
singing bombas, luminarias, piñatas,
Nochebuena, Santa Claus, Papá Noel, los
Reyes Magos; and how her family in the
United States celebrates Christmas.
2. Illustrations are acrylic paint on black
paper.

An Elegy on the Death of César Chávez

Author: Rudolfo Anaya

Illustrator: Gaspar Enriquez

Language: One book in English

Description: 26 pages, color illustrations, 21 ×
26 cm

Published: El Paso, TX: Cinco Puntos Press,
2000

LC#   00024832

Edition:
Cinco Puntos 0938317512 hc.

Summary: This poem eulogizes the Mexican-
American labor activist César Chávez and his
work helping organize migrant farm workers.

Subjects:
American poetry
Chávez, César, 1927–1993—Juvenile poetry
Chávez, César, 1927–1993—Poetry
Children's poetry, American
Labor leaders—Juvenile poetry
Labor leaders—Poetry
Mexican American migrant agricultural
   laborers—Juvenile poetry
Mexican Americans—Juvenile poetry
Mexican Americans—Poetry
Migrant agricultural laborers—Juvenile poetry

Migrant labor—Poetry

English Test:
Accelerated Reader Individual Quiz

Reviewed: *Booklist, School Library Journal*

Awards: Skipping Stones Award, Tomás Rivera

Web site: [students, teachers, parents]
<http://www.ufw.org>

Notes:
1. Dust jacket reverses to a poster chronology of the life of César Chávez.
2. End material includes a summary about the life and work of César Chávez, a chronology, and Anaya's feelings about Chávez.
3. An endnote provides contact information for the United Farm Workers Union and the César Chávez Foundation.

Family, Familia

Author: Diane Gonzales Bertrand

Illustrator: Pauline Rodriguez Howard

Translator: Julia Mercedes Castilla

Language: One bilingual book

Description: 32 pages, color illustrations, 28 cm

Published: Houston, TX: Piñata Books, 1999

LC# 98032227

Editions:
Arte Público 1558852697 hc.
Arte Público 1558852700 pb.

Summary: A reluctant participant in the González family reunion, Daniel has some pleasant surprises and discovers the meaning of family.

Subjects:
Family reunions—Fiction
Mexican Americans—Fiction
Spanish language materials—Bilingual

English Test:
Accelerated Reader Individual Quiz

Spanish Test:
Accelerated Reader *¡Viva Español!*

Reviewed: *Horn Book, Multicultural Review, Publishers Weekly, School Library Journal*

Award: Tomás Rivera

Family Pictures
Cuadros de familia

Author/Illustrator: Carmen Lomas Garza

Translator: Rosalma Zubizarreta

Language: One bilingual book

Description: 30 pages, color illustrations, 22 × 24 cm

Published: San Francisco: Children's Book Press/Libros para niños, 1990

LC#   89027845

Editions:
Children's 0892390506 hc.
Children's 0892391081 pb.
Children's 0892391529 pb. (big edition)

Summary: The author describes, in bilingual text and illustrations, her experiences growing up in a Hispanic community in Texas.

Subjects:
Hispanic American families—Juvenile literature
Hispanic American families—Texas—Kingsville—Juvenile literature
Hispanic Americans—Social life and customs—Juvenile literature
Hispanic Americans—Social life and customs
Hispanic Americans—Texas—Kingsville—Social life and customs—Juvenile literature
Kingsville (Tex.)—Social life and customs—Juvenile literature
Spanish language materials—Bilingual

English Tests:
Accelerated Reader *Trips Through Time, TX Bluebonnet/Lone Star 92/93*
Reading Counts *Literacy Place*; *McGraw-Hill Spotlight on Literacy*

Spanish Tests:
Accelerated Reader *¡Viva Español!*
Reading Counts *Writer Illustrators, Hispanic Authors Collection, Success for All*

Reviewed: *Booklist, Bulletin of the Center for Children's Books, Horn Book, Publishers Weekly, School Library Journal*

Award: Pura Belpré

Lists: ALA Notable Books, Parents' Choice, Scholastic's 200 for 2000, Schon's *Best of the Latino Heritage, 1997*, Texas Bluebonnet Master List 1998–1999

Web site: [parents]
<http://familyhaven.com/parenting/helping/pt6.htmll>

The Farolitos of Christmas

Author: Rudolfo Anaya

Illustrator: Edward Gonzales

Language: One book in English

Description: 40 pages, color illustrations, 29 cm

Published: New York: Hyperion, 1995

LC#   94048073

Editions:
Hyperion 0786820470 lib. bdg.
Hyperion 0786800607 hc.

Summary: With her father away fighting in World War II and her grandfather too sick to create the traditional luminarias, Luz helps create farolitos, little lanterns, for their Christmas celebration instead.

Subjects:
Christmas—Fiction
Grandfathers—Fiction
Mexican Americans—Fiction
New Mexico—Fiction

Reviewed: *Booklist, Horn Book, Publishers Weekly, School Library Journal*

Awards: Américas, Tomás Rivera

List: Schon's *Best of the Latino Heritage, 1997*

Note: A glossary of Spanish words and phrases is included.

Farolitos for Abuelo

Author: Rudolfo Anaya

Illustrator: Edward Gonzales

Language: One book in English

Description: 32 pages, color illustrations, 29 cm

Published: New York: Hyperion, 1998

LC#   97046710

Editions:
Hyperion 0786821868 lib. bdg.
Hyperion 0786802375 hc.

Summary: When Luz's beloved grandfather dies, she places luminaria around his grave on Christmas Eve as a way of remembering him.

Subjects:
Christmas—Fiction
Death—Fiction
Grandfathers—Fiction
Mexican Americans—Fiction
New Mexico—Fiction

Reviewed: *Hungry Mind Review, Kirkus, Publishers Weekly, School Library Journal*

Award: Tomás Rivera

Fiesta U.S.A.

Author and illustrator: George Ancona

Translator: Osvaldo J. Blanco

Language: One book in English and one book in Spanish

Description: 48 pages, color illustrations, 21 × 26 cm

Published: New York: Lodestar/Dutton, 1995

LC#   94034828

Editions:
Lodestar 0525674985 hc.
Lodestar 0525675221 hc. [Spanish]
Continental 9996263479 hc.

Subjects:
Festivals
Festivals—United States—Juvenile literature
Hispanic Americans—Folklore
Hispanic Americans—Social life and customs

Hispanic Americans—Social life and
  customs—Juvenile literature
Holidays
Mexican Americans—Social life and customs
Spanish language materials [Spanish version]
United States—Religious life and customs—
  Juvenile literature
United States—Social life and customs—
  Juvenile literature

English Tests:
  Reading Counts *Nonfiction Featuring
  George Ancona, Holidays and Festivals,
  Biographies and Nonfiction*

Spanish Test:
  Accelerated Reader *¡Viva Español!*

Reviewed: *Booklist, Horn Book, School Library
  Journal*

Award: Américas

Web site:
  [teachers] <http://teacherlink.ed.usu.edu/
  TLresources/longterm/LessonPlans/
  Byrnes/fiesta.html>

Notes:
  1. The book presents four fiestas in San
     Francisco, New Mexico, and New York
     City: Día de los Muertos, Las Posadas,
     Los Matachines, Three Kings' Day
  2. "Papel picado (cut paper) by Rosa María
     Galles."
  3. A glossary is included.
  4. The book begins with an explanation of
     the importance of fiestas as a way of
     preserving traditions of Spanish-speak-
     ing peoples.

Friends from the Other Side
Amigos del otro lado

Author: Gloria Anzaldúa

Illustrator: Consuelo Méndez Castilla

Language: One bilingual book

Description: 28 pages, color illustrations, 26 cm

Published: San Francisco: Children's Book
  Press/Libros para niños, 1993

LC#   92034384

Editions:
  Children's 0892391138 lib. bdg.
  Children's 0892391308 pb.
  Econo-Clad 0613000285 hc.

Summary: Having crossed the Río Grande into
  Texas with his mother in search of a new
  life, Joaquin receives help and friendship
  from Prietita, a brave young Mexican-
  American girl.

Subjects:
  Friendship—Fiction
  Mexican Americans—Fiction
  Spanish language materials—Bilingual
  Texas—Fiction

English Test:
  Reading Counts Individual Quiz

Spanish Test:
  Accelerated Reader *¡Viva Español!*

Reviewed: *Booklist, Horn Book, Kirkus, School Library Journal*

Web sites:
[teachers]
<http://www.yale.edu/ynhti/
curriculum/units/1997/
1/97.01.04.x.html>

<http://humanities-interactive.org/
crossroads/crossroads_la.htm>
<http://education.ucdavis.edu/smr2Lrn/
CI98/Dix_vaca/L_snglGrpMdl.html>

From the Bellybutton of the Moon and Other Summer Poems
Del Ombligo de la Luna y otros poemas de verano

Author: Francisco X. Alarcón

Illustrator: Maya Christina Gonzalez

Language: One bilingual book

Description: 32 pages, color illustrations, 28 cm

Published: San Francisco: Children's Book Press/Libros para niños, 1998

LC# 97037457

Editions:
Children's 0516216473 lib. bdg.
Children's 0892391537 hc.
Children's 0516216961 pb.

Summary: In this bilingual collection of poems, the renowned Mexican-American poet revisits and celebrates his childhood memories of summers, Mexico, and nature.

Subjects:
American poetry
Children's poetry, American
Children's poetry, American—Translations into Spanish
Children's poetry, Hispanic American (Spanish)—Translations into English
Mexico—Juvenile poetry
Mexico—Poetry
Nature—Poetry
Spanish language materials—Bilingual
Summer—Juvenile poetry
Summer—Poetry

English Test:
Reading Counts Individual Quiz

Reviewed: *Booklist, Horn Book, Kirkus, School Library Journal*

Awards: Américas, Pura Belpré, *Skipping Stones* Award, Tomás Rivera

Lists: Children's Choices, Schon's *Recommended Books in Spanish, 1996–1999*

A Gift from Papá Diego
Un regalo de Papá Diego

Author: Benjamin Alire Sáenz

Illustrator: Geronimo Garcia

Language: One bilingual book

Description: 40 pages, color illustrations, 21 × 26 cm

Published: El Paso, TX: Cinco Puntos Press, 1998

LC#   97020640

Editions:
Cinco Puntos 0938317334 pb.
Econo-Clad 0613065875 hc.

Summary: When little Diego gets a Superman outfit for his birthday, he hopes to fly across the border to Mexico to be with his beloved grandfather.

Subjects:
Birthdays—Fiction
Grandfathers—Fiction
Mexican Americans—Fiction
Mexican Americans—Juvenile fiction
Spanish language materials—Bilingual

Spanish Test:
Accelerated Reader *¡Viva Español!*

Reviewed: *Booklist, Hispanic Magazine, Horn Book, Kirkus, Midwest Book Review, People en Español, Publishers Weekly*

Award: Tomás Rivera

Note: Notes and a glossary explain Texas, bilingualism, Spanish terms, and the settling of El Paso.

Grandma Fina and Her Wonderful Umbrellas
La Abuelita Fina y sus sombrillas maravillosas

Author: Benjamin Alire Sáenz

Illustrator: Geronimo Garcia

Translator: Pilar Herrera

Language: One bilingual book

Description: 31 pages, color illustrations, 21 × 27 cm

Published: El Paso, TX: Cinco Puntos Press, 1999

LC#   99014134

Edition:
Cinco Puntos 0938317466 hc.

Summary: After her friends and family all notice that her favorite yellow umbrella is torn, Grandma Fina gets quite a surprise on her birthday.

Subjects:
Birthdays—Fiction

Grandmothers—Fiction
Spanish language materials—Bilingual
Umbrellas and parasols—Fiction

English Test:
Accelerated Reader Individual Quiz

Hairs
Pelitos

Author: Sandra Cisneros

Illustrator: Terry Ybáñez

Translator: Liliana Valenzuela

Language: One bilingual book

Description: 32 pages, color illustrations, 22 cm

Published: New York: Alfred A. Knopf, 1994

LC#   93032775

Editions:
Knopf 0679961712 lib. bdg.
Knopf 0679861718 hc.
Knopf 0679890076 pb.
Econo-Clad 0613051165 hc.

Summary: A girl describes how each person in the family has hair that looks and acts different: Papa's like a broom, Kiki's like fur, and Mama's with the sweet smell of bread before it's baked.

Subjects:
Hair—Fiction
Hispanic Americans—Fiction
Mothers and daughters—Fiction
Spanish language materials—Bilingual

Spanish Test:
Accelerated Reader *¡Viva Español!*

Reviewed: *Booklist, Bulletin of the Center for Children's Books, Horn Book, Kirkus, Publishers Weekly*

List: Parents' Choice

Web site: [teachers]
<http://www.mprojects.wiu.edu/ei/hair.html>

Note: This picture book is based on a chapter from *The House on Mango Street*.

Hooray! A Piñata!
Viva! Una piñata!

Author and illustrator: Elisa Kleven

Translator: Lidia Díaz

Language: One book in English and one book in Spanish

Description: 30 pages, color illustrations, 29 cm

Published: New York: Dutton Children's Books, 1996

LC#   95045750 [English]
     96024577 [Spanish]

English Editions:
   Dutton 0525456058 hc.
   Puffin 014056764X pb.

Spanish Edition:
   Dutton 0525456066 hc.

Summary: After she chooses a cute dog piñata for her birthday party, Clara pretends it is her pet, and she doesn't want it to get broken.

Subjects:
   Dogs—Fiction
   Hispanic Americans—Fiction
   Parties—Fiction
   Piñatas—Fiction
   Spanish language materials
      [Spanish version]

English Test:
   Accelerated Reader *Fables, Fantasies & Fun*

Spanish Test:
   Accelerated Reader *¡Viva Español!*

Reviewed: *Booklist, Horn Book, Publishers Weekly, School Library Journal*

Award: Américas

Lists: *Booklist* Editors' Choice, Schon's *Recommended Books in Spanish, 1996–1999*

Web site: [Parents and teachers]
   <http://pages.ripco.net/~esme/unbirthday.html>

Icy Watermelon
Sandía fría

Author: Mary Sue Galindo

Illustrator: Pauline Rodriguez Howard

Language: One bilingual book

Description: 32 pages, color illustrations, 28 cm

Published: Houston, TX: Piñata Books, 2000

LC#   00035604

Edition:
   Arte Público 1558853065 hc.

Summary: When three generations of a family gather to eat watermelon, the grandparents reminisce about how the sweet fruit brought them together.

Subjects:
Grandparents—Fiction
Mexican Americans—Fiction
Spanish language materials—Bilingual
Watermelon—Fiction

English Test:
Accelerated Reader Individual Quiz

Spanish Test:
Accelerated Reader Individual Quiz

Reviewed: *Booklist, Críticas, School Library Journal*

Award: Tomás Rivera

In My Family: Paintings and Stories by Carmen Lomas Garza
En mi familia: Cuadros y relatos de Carmen Lomas Garza

Author and illustrator: Carmen Lomas Garza

Editors: Harriet Rohmer and David Schecter

Translator: Francisco X. Alarcón

Language: One bilingual book

Description: 32 pages, color illustrations, 23 × 26 cm

Published: San Francisco: Children's Book Press/Libros Para Niños, 1996

LC# 96007471

Editions:
Children's 0892391383 hc.
Children's 0892391634 pb.

Summary: The author describes, in bilingual text and illustrations, her experiences growing up in a Hispanic community in Texas.

Subjects:
Hispanic American families—Juvenile literature

Hispanic American families—Texas—Kingsville—Juvenile literature
Hispanic Americans—Social life and customs
Hispanic Americans—Social life and customs—Juvenile literature
Hispanic Americans—Texas—Kingsville—Social life and customs—Juvenile literature
Kingsville (Tex.)—Social life and customs
Lomas Garza, Carmen—Childhood and youth—Juvenile literature
Spanish language materials—Bilingual

EnglishTests:
Accelerated Reader *TX Bluebonnet/ Lone Star 98/99*
Reading Counts Individual Quiz

Spanish Tests:
Accelerated Reader *¡Viva Español!*
Reading Counts *Showcase on Newberry & Other Awards, Hispanic Authors Collection, Me and My Family*

Reviewed: *Booklist, Horn Book, School Library Journal*

Awards: Américas, Pura Belpré, *Skipping Stones*, Tomás Rivera

Lists: Notable Books for a Global Society, Schon's *Recommended Books in Spanish, 1996-1999*, Teachers' Choice, Texas Bluebonnet Master List 1997-1998

Web sites: [teachers]
<http://www.pgcps.org/~lessons/En%20Mi%20Familia/en_mi_familia.htm>
<http://mati.eas.asu.edu:8421/ChicanArte/html_pages/Protest.L4-PrintM.html>

Isla
La isla

Author: Arthur Dorros

Illustrator: Elisa Kleven

Translator: Sandra Marulanda Dorros

Language: One book in English and one book in Spanish

Description: 40 pages, color illustrations, 28 cm

Published: New York: Dutton Children's Books, 1995

LC# 94040900 [English]
        95014705 [Spanish]

English Editions:
Dutton 0525451498 hc.
Puffin 0140565418 pb.
Econo-Clad 0613148657 lib. bdg.

Spanish Editions:
Dutton 0525454225 hc.
Puffin 0140565051 pb.
Econo-Clad 0613182588 lib. bdg.

Summary: A young girl and her grandmother take an imaginary journey to the Caribbean island where her mother grew up and where some of her family still lives.

Subjects:
Caribbean Area—Fiction
Grandmothers—Fiction
Hispanic Americans—Fiction
Islands—Fiction
Spanish language materials [Spanish version]

Spanish Test:
Accelerated Reader *¡Viva Español!*

Reviewed: *Booklist, Horn Book, Publishers Weekly, School Library Journal*

Award: Américas

Web sites: [teachers]
<http://www.murrieta.k12.ca.us/alta/grade3/isla/>
<http://teacherlink.ed.usu.edu/TLresources/longterm/LessonPlans/socst/moser/moser.html>

Note: This book is a continuation of *Abuela*.

It Doesn't Have to Be This Way: A Barrio Story
No tiene que ser así: Una historia del barrio

Author: Luis J. Rodríguez

Illustrator: Daniel Galvez

Language: One bilingual book

Description: 32 pages, color illustrations, 28 cm

Published: San Francisco: Children's Book Press/Libros para niños, 1999

LC# 98056507

Edition:
Children's 0892391618 hc.

Summary: Reluctantly, a young boy becomes more and more involved in the activities of a local gang, until a tragic event involving his cousin forces him to make a choice about the course of his life.

Subjects:
Gangs—Fiction
Hispanic Americans—Fiction

Spanish language materials—Bilingual

Spanish Test:
Accelerated Reader Individual Quiz

Reviewed: *Booklist, Horn Book, Kirkus, Multicultural Review, Publishers Weekly*

Awards: Américas, *Skipping Stones*, Tomás Rivera

Lists: Parents' Choice, *Smithsonian* Notable Books for Children

Notes:
1. Pages two and three contain an introduction in which the author tells about his own involvement with gangs and points out the reasons young people join gangs. They also contain photographs of Rodríguez as an 11-year-old gang member, as an adult, and with his family.
2. The main character, Monchi (Ramon), likes to read and write poetry.

Laughing Tomatoes and Other Spring Poems
Jitomates Risueños y otros poemas de primavera

Author: Francisco X. Alarcón

Illustrator: Maya Christina Gonzalez

Language: One bilingual book

Description: 32 pages, color illustrations, 28 cm

Published: San Francisco: Children's Book Press/Libros para niños, 1997
LC# 96007459

Editions:
Children's 0516205455 lib. bdg.
Children's 0892391391 hc.
Econo-Clad 0613070100 hc.

Summary: This is a bilingual collection of humorous and serious poems about family, nature, and celebrations by a renowned Mexican-American poet.

Subjects:
American poetry
Children's poetry, American
Children's poetry, American—Translations into Spanish
Children's poetry, Hispanic American (Spanish)—Translations into English
Nature—Juvenile poetry
Nature—Poetry
Spanish language materials—Bilingual
Spring—Juvenile poetry
Spring—Poetry

English Test:
Reading Counts *Multicultural Titles, Literacy Place*

Reviewed: *Booklist, Horn Book, Kirkus, Multicultural Review, School Library Journal*

Awards: Américas, National Parenting Publications Gold Award, Pura Belpré, Tomás Rivera

List: Schon's *Recommended Books in Spanish, 1996–1999*

Liliana's Grandmothers
Las abuelas de Liliana

Author and illustrator: Leyla Torres

Language: One book in English and one book in Spanish

Description: 32 pages, color illustrations, 27 cm

Published: New York: Farrar Straus Giroux, 1998

LC#　97037256 [English]
　　　　97037245 [Spanish]

English Edition:
Farrar 0374351058 hc.

Spanish Edition:
Farrar 0374343411 hc.

Summary: Because one of her grandmothers lives down the street and the other in a far-away country, Liliana experiences two different ways of life when she visits them.

Subjects:
Grandmothers—Fiction
Spanish language materials [Spanish version]

English Test:
Accelerated Reader *Readers on Parade, GA Book Awards 99/00*

Spanish Test:
Accelerated Reader *¡Viva Español!*

Reviewed: *Booklist, Horn Book, Kirkus, School Library Journal*

Award: Américas

List: Schon's *Recommended Books in Spanish, 1996–1999*

Note: Liliana's teddy bear accompanies her and appears in each illustration.

Magda's Tortillas
Las tortillas de Magda

Author: Becky Chavarría-Cháirez

Illustrator: Anne Vega

Translator: Julia Mercedes Castilla

Language: One bilingual book

Description: 32 pages, color illustrations, 28 cm

Published: Houston, TX: Piñata Books, 2000

LC# 99046433

Editions:
Arte Público 1558852867 hc.
Arte Público 1558852875 pb.

Summary: While learning to make tortillas on her seventh birthday, Magda tries to make perfectly round ones like those made by her grandmother, but instead creates a variety of wonderful shapes.

Subjects:
Birthdays—Fiction
Cookery, Mexican—Fiction
Grandmothers—Fiction
Shape—Fiction
Spanish language materials—Bilingual
Tortillas—Fiction

English Tests:
Accelerated Reader Individual Quiz
Reading Counts Individual Quiz

Spanish Test:
Accelerated Reader Individual Quiz

Reviewed: *Booklist, Críticas*

Award: Tomás Rivera

Magic Windows
Ventanas mágicas

Author and illustrator: Carmen Lomas Garza

Editors: Harriet Rohmer and David Schecter

Translator: Francisco X. Alarcón

Language: One bilingual book

Description: 32 pages, color illustrations, 28 cm

Published: San Francisco: Children's Book Press/Libros para niños, 1999

LC# 98038379

Editions:
Children's 089239157X hc.

Summary: In Spanish and English, Carmen Lomas Garza portrays her family's Mexican customs through cut-paper work.

Subjects:
Handicraft
Lomas Garza, Carmen
Lomas Garza, Carmen—Family—Juvenile

literature
Mexican American families—Juvenile
literature
Mexican Americans—Social life and
customs—Juvenile literature
Mexico—Social life and customs
Mexico—Social life and customs—Juvenile
literature
Paper work
Paper work—Juvenile literature
Spanish language materials—Bilingual—
Juvenile literature

English Tests:
Accelerated Reader *Rays of Sunshine*
Reading Counts Individual Quiz

Reviewed: *Horn Book, Hungry Mind, Parents'
Choice, School Library Journal*

Awards: Américas, Carter G. Woodson Award,
Pura Belpré, *Skipping Stones*, Tomás Rivera

List: Parents' Choice

Mama Provi and the Pot of Rice

Author: Sylvia Rosa-Casanova

Illustrator: Robert Roth

Language: One book in English

Description: unpaged, color illustrations, 26 cm

Published: New York: Atheneum Books for
Young Readers, 1997

LC# 95044677

Edition:
Atheneum 0689319320 lib. bdg.

Summary: Mama Provi takes chicken and rice
to her sick granddaughter Lucy, who lives
upstairs.

Subjects:
Chickenpox—Fiction

Food—Fiction
Grandmothers—Fiction
Hispanic Americans—Fiction

English Tests:
Accelerated Reader *CA Young Reader Medal
99/00, GA Book Award 00/01, NC
Children's Book Award 00/01*
Reading Counts *CA Young Reader Medal
1999–2000, GA Picture Storybook Award
2000–2001*

Reviewed: *Booklist, Bulletin of the Center for
Children's Books, Horn Book, Kirkus, New
York Times Book Review, Publishers Weekly,
School Library Journal*

Lists: California Young Reader Medal Reading
List, Georgia Book Award Nominees, North
Carolina Children's Book Award Nominees

La Mariposa

Author: Francisco Jiménez

Illustrator: Simón Silva

Language: One book in English and one book in Spanish

Description: 40 pages, color illustrations, 26 cm

Published: Boston: Houghton Mifflin, 1998

LC# 96027664

English Editions:
Houghton 0395816637 hc.
Houghton 0618073175 pb.

Spanish Editions:
Houghton 0395917387 hc.
Houghton 0618070362 pb.

Summary: Because he can speak only Spanish, Francisco, son of a migrant worker, has trouble when he begins first grade, but his fascination with the caterpillar in the classroom helps him begin to fit in.

Subjects:
Mexican Americans—Fiction
Schools—Fiction
Spanish language materials [Spanish version]

Spanish Test:
Accelerated Reader *¡Viva Español!*

Reviewed: *Booklist, Horn Book, Kirkus, Parents Choice, Publishers Weekly, School Library Journal*

Awards: Américas, Tomás Rivera

List: *Smithsonian* Notable Books for Children

Note: Illustrations are gouache on illustration board.

My Aunt Otilia's Spirits
Los espíritus de mi Tía Otilia

Author: Richard García

Illustrators: Robin Cherin and Roger I. Reyes

Translator: Jesús Guerrero Rea

Language: One bilingual book

Description: 24 pages, color illustrations, 25 cm

Published: San Francisco: Children's Book Press/Libros para niños, 1987

LC# 86017129

Edition:
Children's 0892390298 lib. bdg. [revised edition]

Series: *Fifth World Tales (Cuentos del quinto mundo)*

Summary: The wall knockings and bed shakings that always accompany Aunt Otilia's visits do not bother a young boy until the night he sees her skeleton leave her body.

Revised edition summary: When tall, skinny Aunt Otilia comes to visit from Puerto Rico, her curious nephew finds out about her magical powers.

Subjects:
Aunts—Fiction
Parapsychology—Fiction
Puerto Ricans—United States—Fiction
Spanish language—Readers

Spanish language materials—Bilingual

Reviewed: *Booklist*

Notes:
1. On page 24 "The author talks about his story."
2. This is one of the earliest picture books to feature an original story with Puerto Rican characters.

My Very Own Room
Mi propio cuartito

Author: Amada Irma Pérez

Illustrator: Maya Christina Gonzalez

Language: One bilingual book

Description: 32 pages, color illustrations, 26 cm

Published: San Francisco: Children's Book Press/Libros para niños, 2000

LC# 00020769

Edition:
Children's 0892391642 hc.

Summary: With the help of her family, a resourceful Mexican-American girl realizes her dream of having a space of her own to read and to think.

Subjects:
Bedrooms—Fiction
Family life—Fiction
Mexican Americans—Fiction
Spanish language materials—Bilingual

English Test:
Accelerated Reader Individual Quiz

Spanish Test:
Accelerated Reader Individual Quiz

Reviewed: *Booklist, Horn Book, Publishers Weekly, School Library Journal*

Awards: *Skipping Stones* Award, Tomás Rivera

Los Ojos del Tejedor
The Eyes of the Weaver

Author: Cristina Ortega

Illustrator: Patricio García

Language: One book in English with Spanish phrases

Description: 64 pages, color illustrations, 26 cm

Published: Santa Fe, NM: Clear Light Publishers, 1996

LC# 96011137

Edition:
Clear Light 0940666812 pb.

Summary: Ten-year-old María Cristina goes to visit her grandfather so that he can teach her to weave, as her family in northern New Mexico has done for seven generations.

Subjects:
Grandfathers—Fiction

Mexican Americans—Fiction
New Mexico—Fiction
Weaving—Fiction

English Test:
Accelerated Reader Individual Quiz

Reviewed: *Midwest Book Review*

Notes:
1. A glossary of Spanish words and phrases is included.
2. This book is based on experiences of the author and her grandfather, whose works are included in the "American Encounters" exhibit at the National Museum of American History in the Smithsonian Institution in Washington, D.C.

Pablo's Tree

Author: Pat Mora

Illustrator: Cecily Lang

Language: One book in English

Description: 32 pages, color illustrations, 25 cm

Published: New York: Simon & Schuster, 1994

LC# 92027145

Edition:
Simon & Schuster 0027674010 lib. bdg.

Summary: Each year on his birthday, a young Mexican-American boy looks forward to seeing how his grandfather has decorated the tree he planted on the day the boy was adopted.

Subjects:
Adoption—Fiction
Birthdays—Fiction

Grandfathers—Fiction
Mexican Americans—Fiction

English Tests:
 Accelerated Reader Individual Quiz
 Reading Counts *Hispanic Experience for K–2, Harcourt Brace Signatures,*

Harcourt Brace Stories in Time, SBG Literature Work, Literacy Place

Reviewed: *Booklist, Bulletin of the Center for Children's Books, Horn Book, Kirkus*

Award: Américas

Pepita Takes Time
Pepita, siempre tarde

Author: Ofelia Dumas Lachtman

Illustrator: Alex Pardo DeLange

Translator: Alejandra Balestra

Language: One bilingual book

Description: 32 pages, color illustrations, 28 cm

Published: Houston, TX: Piñata Books, 2000

LC#   00035641

Editions:
 Arte Público 1558853049 hc.
 Arte Público 1558853073 pb.

Summary: Pepita thinks it doesn't matter that she is always late, until she finally realizes how her tardiness affects other people and herself.

Subjects:
 Behavior—Fiction
 Hispanic Americans—Fiction
 Interpersonal relations—Fiction
 Spanish language materials—Bilingual
 Tardiness—Fiction

English Test:
 Accelerated Reader Individual Quiz

Spanish Test:
 Accelerated Reader Individual Quiz

Reviewed: *School Library Journal*

Award: Tomás Rivera

Pepita Talks Twice
Pepita habla dos veces

Author: Ofelia Dumas Lachtman

Illustrator: Alex Pardo DeLange

Language: One bilingual book

Description: 32 pages, color illustrations, 28 cm

Published: Houston, TX: Piñata Books, 1995

LC# 95009869

Edition:
Arte Público 1558850775 hc.

Summary: Pepita, a little girl who can converse in Spanish and in English, decides not to "speak twice" until unanticipated problems cause her to think twice about her decision.

Subjects:
Bilingualism—Fiction
Decision making—Fiction
Hispanic Americans—Fiction
Spanish language materials—Bilingual

Spanish Test:
Accelerated Reader *¡Viva Español!*

Reviewed: *Horn Book*

Awards: *Skipping Stones*, Tomás Rivera

Pepita Thinks Pink
Pepita y el color rosado

Author: Ofelia Dumas Lachtman

Illustrator: Alex Pardo DeLange

Translator: Yanitzia Canetti

Language: One bilingual book

Description: 32 pages, color illustrations, 28 cm

Published: Houston, TX: Piñata Books, 1998

LC# 97029676

Editions:
Arte Público 1558852220 hc.
Arte Público 1558852409 pb.

Summary: Pepita does not like the color pink and is dismayed to learn that it is the favorite color of the pink little girl who moves in next door.

Subjects:
Color—Fiction
Friendship—Fiction
Mexican Americans—Fiction
Pink—Fiction
Prejudices—Fiction
Spanish language materials—Bilingual

Spanish Test:
Accelerated Reader *¡Viva Español!*

Reviewed: *Horn Book*

Award: Tomás Rivera

The Piñata Quilt

Author and illustrator: Jane Tenorio-Coscarelli

Language: One book in English

Description: 47 pages, color illustrations, 29 cm

Published: Murrieta, CA: Quarter Inch Designs & Publishing, 1999

LC# 99064894

Editions:
Quarter Inch 0965342255 hc.
Quarter Inch 0965342263 pb.

Summary: Albert's birthday party involves a piñata with too much glue.

Subjects:
Birthdays—Fiction
Hispanic Americans—Fiction
Piñatas—Fiction
Quilting—Fiction

Award: Tomás Rivera

Notes:
1. This book is written in English with some Spanish words printed below the English text.
2. Directions and patterns for making a piñata and a piñata quilt are included.
3. Each illustration includes a tiny gray mouse.

Radio Man
Don Radio
A Story in English and Spanish

Author and illustrator: Arthur Dorros

Translator: Sandra Marulanda Dorros

Language: One bilingual book

Description: 40 pages, color illustrations, 23 × 26 cm

Published: New York: HarperCollins, 1997

LC# 92028369

Editions:
Harper 0064434826 pb.
Econo-Clad 0613057481 hc.

Summary: As he travels with his family of migrant farmworkers, Diego relies on his radio to provide him with companionship and to help connect him to all the different places in which he lives.

Subjects:
Mexican Americans—Fiction
Migrant labor—Fiction
Radio—Fiction
Spanish language materials—Bilingual

English Test:
Reading Counts *Hispanic Experience for K–2*

Spanish Tests:
Accelerated Reader *¡Viva Español!*
Reading Counts *Friends & My Community for K–2, Showcase on Diversity, Success for All*

Reviewed: *Booklist, Horn Book, Publishers Weekly, School Library Journal*

Award: Américas

Web site: [students]
<http://horizon.nmsu.edu/ddl/wqharvest.html>

Notes:
1. A glossary and pronunciation guide for Spanish words and phrases are included.
2. Illustrations were painted with acrylics.

The Rainbow Tulip

Author: Pat Mora

Illustrator: Elizabeth Sayles

Language: One book in English

Description: 32 pages, color illustrations, 26 cm

Published: New York, Viking, 1999

LC# 98015868

Edition:
Viking 0670872911 hc.

Summary: A Mexican-American first grader experiences the difficulties and pleasures of being different when she wears a tulip costume with all the colors of the rainbow for the school May Day parade.

Subjects:
May Day—Fiction
Mexican Americans—Fiction
Mexican Americans—Juvenile fiction
Schools—Fiction

English Tests:
Accelerated Reader *Happily Ever After*
Reading Counts Individual Quiz

Reviewed: *Booklist, Horn Book, Kirkus, Publishers Weekly, School Library Journal*

Award: Tomás Rivera

List: California Department of Education Recommended Literature List

Web site: [teachers]
<http://www.coe.ufl.edu/faculty/lamme/book/RealisticFictionArticles/TheRainbowTulipA.html>

Salsa

Author: Lillian Colón-Vilá

Illustrator: Roberta Collier-Morales

Language: One bilingual book

Description: 32 pages, color illustrations, 22 × 29 cm

Published: Houston, TX: Piñata Books, 1998

LC# 97023305

Editions:
>Arte Público 1558852204 hc.
>Arte Público 1558852387 pbk.

Summary: Rita, a young girl living in New York's El Barrio, describes the Afro-Caribbean dance music, salsa, and imagines being a salsa orchestra director.

Subjects:
>Hispanic Americans—Fiction
>Salsa (Music)—Fiction
>Spanish language materials—Bilingual

Spanish Test:
>Accelerated Reader *¡Viva Español!*

Reviewed: *Horn Book*

Sip, Slurp, Soup, Soup
Caldo, caldo, caldo

Author: Diane Gonzales Bertrand

Illustrator: Alex Pardo DeLange

Language: One bilingual book

Description: 30 pages, color illustrations, 22 cm

Published: Houston, TX: Piñata Books, 1996

LC# 96044383

Edition:
>Arte Público 1558851836 hc.

Summary: A rhythmic text with repetitive phrases relates how the children watch Mamá make soup and go with Papá to get tortillas before enjoying the results of her labor.

Subjects:
>Family life—Fiction
>Mexican Americans—Fiction
>Soups—Fiction
>Spanish language materials—Bilingual
>Tortillas—Fiction

Spanish Test:
>Accelerated Reader *¡Viva Español!*

Reviewed: *Horn Book, Publishers Weekly, School Library Journal*

Award: Tomás Rivera

Note: A recipe for caldo is included.

Snapshots from the Wedding

Author: Gary Soto

Illustrator: Stephanie Garcia

Language: One book in English

Description: 32 pages, color illustrations, 26 cm

Published: New York: G. P. Putnam's Sons, 1997

LC# 95005793

Editions:
Putnam's 039922808X lib. bdg.
Paper Star 0698117522 pb.
Econo-Clad 0613121171 hc.

Summary: Maya, the flower girl, describes a Mexican-American wedding through snapshots of the day's events, beginning with the procession to the altar and ending with her sleeping after the dance.

Subjects:
Mexican Americans—Fiction
Weddings—Fiction

English Test:
Reading Counts Individual Quiz

Reviewed: *Booklist, Bulletin of the Center for Children's Books, Horn Book, Kirkus, Publishers Weekly, School Library Journal*

Awards: Pura Belpré, Tomás Rivera

Lists: *Booklist* Editors' Choice, *Bulletin of the Center for Children's Books* Blue Ribbon Books

Subway Sparrow
Gorrión del metro

Author and illustrator: Leyla Torres

Language: One book in English and one book in Spanish.

Description: 32 pages, color illustrations, 24 × 28 cm

Published: New York: Farrar, Straus, Giroux, 1993

LC# 92055104 [English]
93000511 [Spanish]

English Editions:
Farrar 0374372853 hc.
Farrar 0374471290 pb.
Econo-Clad 0613024893 hc.

Spanish Editions:
Farrar 0374327564 hc.
Farrar 0374427828 pb.

Summary: Although the passengers of the D train speak different languages, they work together to rescue a frightened bird.

Subjects:
Birds—Fiction
Polyglot materials
Spanish language materials [Spanish version]
Subways—Fiction

English Test:
Accelerated Reader Individual Quiz

Spanish Test:
Accelerated Reader *¡Viva Español!*

Reviewed: *Booklist, Horn Book, Kirkus*

List: Schon's *Recommended Books in Spanish, 1991–1995*

The Tamale Quilt

Author and illustrator: Jane Tenorio-Coscarelli

Language: One book in English

Description: 47 pages, color illustrations, 28 cm

Published: Quarter Inch Designs & Publishing, 1998

LC# 98091732

Editions:
Quarter Inch 0965342239 hc.
Quarter Inch 0965342247 pb.

Summary: Grandma shares her recipe for making tamales, a traditional food of the Christmas season. A recipe and a pattern for the tamale quilt are included.

Subjects:
Christmas—Fiction
Grandmothers—Fiction
Hispanic Americans—Fiction
Quilting—Fiction

Award: Tomás Rivera

Notes:
1. Each illustration includes a tiny, gray mouse.
2. Appliqué patterns for husk, hand, heart, olive, corn, and corn leaves are included.

Tomás and the Library Lady
Tomás y la señora de la biblioteca

Author: Pat Mora

Illustrator: Raul Colón

Translator: Amy Prince

Language: One book in English and one book in Spanish

Description: 40 pages, color illustrations, 26 cm

Published: New York, Dragonfly Books/Alfred A. Knopf, 1997

LC# 89037490 [English]
89037490 [English]
97004280 [Spanish]

English Editions:
Knopf 0679904018 lib. bdg.
Knopf 0679804013 hc.
Dragonfly 0375803491 pb.

Spanish Editions:
Dragonfly 0679941738 lib. bdg.
Dragonfly 06798417733 pb.
David McKay 0679841733 pb.
Econo-Clad 061306058X hc.

Summary: While helping his family in their work as migrant laborers far from their home, Tomás finds an entire world to explore in the books at the local public library.

Subjects:
Books and reading—Fiction
Libraries—Fiction
Mexican Americans—Fiction

Migrant labor—Fiction
Spanish language materials [Spanish version]

English Tests:
Accelerated Reader *Folktales and Freedom*;
GA Book Award 00/01; NE *Golden
Sower*; *PA Young Reader's Choice 99/00*;
TX Bluebonnet/Lone Star 1999/2000; *UT
Children's Award 00/01*
Reading Counts *TX Bluebonnet Award
1999–2000*; *PA Young Reader's Choice
K–3 1999–2000*; *GA Picture Storybook
Award 2000–2001*

Spanish Test:
Accelerated Reader *¡Viva Español!*

Reviewed: *Booklist, Críticas, Horn Book,
Kirkus, Publishers Weekly, School Library
Journal*

Awards: Américas, *Skipping Stones*, Tomás
Rivera

Lists: California Department of Education,
Georgia Book Award Nominees, Nebraska
Golden Sower Award Nominees,
Pennsylvania Young Readers' Choice,
Scholastic 200 for 2000, Schon's
*Recommended Books in Spanish,
1996–1999, Smithsonian* Notable Books for
Children, Texas Bluebonnet Master List
1999–2000

Web site: [librarians]
<http://www.tdo.com/features/families/
library/0421library.htm>

Too Many Tamales
Qué montón de tamales!

Author: Gary Soto

Illustrator: Ed Martínez

Translators: Alma Flor Ada and F. Isabel
Campoy

Language: One book in English and one book
in Spanish

Description: 30 pages, color illustrations, 29 cm

English Publisher: New York: Putnam, 1993

LC# 91019229 [English]
96010474 [Spanish]

English Editions:
Putnam 0399221468 lib. bdg.

Paper Star 0698114124 pb.
Econo-Clad 0613004051 hc.

Spanish Edition:
PaperStar 0698114132 pb.

Summary: María tries on her mother's wedding
ring while helping make tamales for a
Christmas family get-together. Hours later,
panic ensues when she realizes the ring is
missing.

Subjects:
Christmas—Fiction
Mexican Americans—Fiction
Rings—Fiction
Spanish language materials [Spanish
version]

English Tests:
    Accelerated Reader *Bonanza of Books*
    Reading Counts *Hispanic Experience for
        K–2, Lucky Book Club, Literacy Place,
        Success for All, SRC Multicultural
        Grades 2–3*

Spanish Tests:
    Accelerated Reader *¡Viva Español!*
    Reading Counts *Hispanic Authors
        Collection, Me and My Family for K–2,
        Showcase on Diversity K–2*

Reviewed: *Booklist, Bulletin of the Center for
    Children's Books, Horn Book, Kirkus,
    Publishers Weekly, School Library Journal*

Lists: California Department of Education,
    Schon's *Recommended Books in Spanish,
    1996–1999*

Web sites:
    [teachers and students]
        <http://www.sdcoe.k12.ca.us/score/too/
            toosg4.html>
    [teachers]
        <http://mcps.k12.md.us/curriculum/
            socialstd/MBD/Too_Tamales2.html>
        <http://www.courses.dsu.edu/eled360/
            michelle/index.html>
        <http://www.sdcoe.k12.ca.us/score/too/
            tootg.html>

The Tortilla Quilt

Author and illustrator: Jane Tenorio-Coscarelli

Language: One book in English

Description: 47 pages, color illustrations, 29 cm

Published: Murrieta, CA: Quarter Inch Designs
    and Publishing, 1996

LC#   96092477

Editions:
    Quarter Inch 0965342204 hc.
    Quarter Inch 0965342212 pb.

Summary: On a ranch in the 1880s,
    Grandmother Lupita teaches her grand-
    daughter María to make a quilt from flour
    sacks and old clothes.

Subjects:
    Grandmothers—Fiction
    Hispanic Americans—Fiction
    Quilting—Fiction

Award: Tomás Rivera

Web site: [teachers]
    <http://www.hgtv.com/HGTV/project/
        0,1158,CRHO_project_3800,FF.html>

Notes:
1. A recipe and a pattern for the tortilla
   quilt are included.
2. A tiny, gray mouse hides within each
   illustration.
3. Text is in English with some Spanish
   words printed beneath their English
   equivalents.

The Upside Down Boy
El niño de cabeza

Author: Juan Felipe Herrera

Illustrator: Elizabeth Gómez

Language: One bilingual book

Description: 32 pages, color illustrations, 26 cm

Published: San Francisco: Children's Book Press/Libros para niños, 2000

LC#   99049113

Edition:
Children's 0892391626 hc.

Summary: The author recalls the year when his farm worker parents settled down in the city so that he could go to school for the first time.

Subjects:
Herrera, Juan Felipe—Childhood and youth

Herrera, Juan Felipe—Childhood and youth—Juvenile literature
Mexican American poets—Biography—Juvenile literature
Poets, American
Poets, American—20th century—Biography—Juvenile literature
Spanish language materials—Bilingual

English Tests:
Accelerated Reader *Fairy Tales and Fables, TX Bluebonnet/Lone Star*
Reading Counts *TX Bluebonnet Award 2001–02*

Reviewed: *School Library Journal*

Award: Tomás Rivera

List: Texas Bluebonnet Master List 2001–2001

Note: This book is a sequel to *Calling the Doves.*

When This World Was New
Un mundo nuevo

Author: D. H. Figueredo

Illustrator: Enrique O. Sánchez

Translator: Eida de la Vega

Language: One book in English and one book in Spanish

Description: 32 pages, color illustrations, 27 cm

Published: New York: Lee & Low Books, 1999

LC#   98053068 [English]
00032739 [Spanish]

English Edition:
Lee & Low 1880000865 hc.

Spanish Editions:
Lee & Low 158430006X hc.
Lee & Low 1584300078 pb.

Summary: When his father leads him on a magical trip of discovery through new fallen snow, a young boy who emigrated from his warm island home overcomes fears about living in New York.

Subjects:
Emigration and immigration—Fiction
Fathers and sons—Fiction
Fear—Fiction
Snow—Fiction
Spanish language materials [Spanish version]

English Tests:
Accelerated Reader *Multicultural Library (Lee & Low), Books Are Fun Elementary* Reading Counts Individual Quiz

Reviewed: *Booklist, Horn Book, Kirkus, Publishers Weekly, School Library Journal*

Web site: [teachers]
<http://www.coe.ufl.edu/faculty/lamme/book/PictureBooksArticles/WhenThisWorldWasNew.html>

Note: Illustrations are acrylic on paper.

Authors, Illustrators, and Translators

This section contains biographical and career information about the writers, artists, and translators of books listed in Part II. These individuals represent excellence in their fields, and students are encouraged to consider the careers and accomplishments of these individuals when thinking of future occupations. Bilingual individuals should consider translating as a career option. Persons who enjoy storytelling may wish to enter the field of writing, and book illustration is an admirable use of artistic and creative talent.

Most of the biographical information was taken from book jackets or author information pages in the picture books. Some publication data was taken from the Library of Congress. Some facts were obtained from Web pages. When information was taken from resources other than these, that fact has been noted.

Available Web sites are listed after each entry for the reader's convenience, whether or not they were consulted in the compiling of biographical data. With advances in computer technology have come opportunities for malicious manipulation of that technology. Web sites listed herein are legitimate at this time. However, it is recommended that readers check these sites for possible inappropriate changes before recommending them to others.

Reference books such as *Authors and Artists for Young Adults*, *Contemporary Authors*, *Dictionary of Literary Biography*, and *Something About the Author* are listed in "For Further Reading" at the end of this section. Those desiring to learn more are encouraged to consult their local school, university, or public libraries.

Anthony Accardo

Illustrator

Anthony Accardo was born in New York City, but grew up in Italy, where he studied art. He earned a degree in art and advertising design from New York City Technical College. Since 1987 he has been a member of the Society of Illustrators. His art has been exhibited in Europe as well as in the United States. In addition to *Benito's Bizcochitos*, Accardo has illustrated more than 50 picture books, including the *Nancy Drew Notebooks* series. His drawings illustrate Pat Mora's *My Own True Name*, a book of poems for young adults. He lives in Brooklyn, New York, but frequently travels.

<http://illustration.homestead.com/bio.html>

Alma Flor Ada

Author, illustrator, and translator

Alma Flor Ada was born in 1938 in Camagüey, Cuba. Her grandmother taught her to read when she was three years old. Her grandmother and an uncle were storytellers, so she was exposed to stories and literature at an early age. She earned a Ph.D. in Spanish literature from the Pontifical Catholic University of Lima. Her works have been published in Argentina, Peru, Spain, and Mexico. Founder of the *Journal of the National Association for Bilingual Education*, Ada has been active in professional associations and is on the advisory board of the Children's Television Workshop.

A professor at the University of San Francisco since 1976, she is Director of the Center for Multicultural Literature for Children and Young Adults. Ada is the mother of four children and grandmother of three. Her autobiography, *Under the Royal Palms: A Childhood in Cuba*, was published in 1998 (*Something*, vol. 84).

<http://www.almaflorada.net/> <http://teacher.scholastic.com/writewit/folk/bio.htm>

Francisco X. Alarcón (Francisco Xavier Alarcón)

Author

A well-known poet, Alarcón was born in 1954 in Wilmington, California. He grew up in the United States and Mexico, and attended East Los Angeles College, California State University, Stanford University, and Universidad Nacional Autonoma de Mexico. He has published several other books of poetry in Swedish, Irish, English, and Spanish, and his poetry has appeared in many anthologies. Alarcón is a part of the Children's Book Press LitLink Project, through which he visits schools and shares his poetry.

He believes that poetry can improve reading skills and encourage imagination. His books help Mexican-American children see themselves in stories and help readers from other backgrounds understand more about Latino culture. He lives in Davis, California, where he is a teacher and director of the Spanish for Native Speakers program at the University of California (*Something*, vol. 104).

<http://dcn.davis.ca.us/go/gizmo/1997/alarcon.html>

Juanita Alba

Author

Juanita Alba has worked as a bilingual elementary teacher and an administrator with departments of education in the states of Washington and Texas. A resident of Austin, Texas, she is a technology consultant. She works with school districts, regional educational service centers, and universities in integrating technology. Alba was on the writing team of the Technology Applications portion of the Texas Essential Knowledge and Skills of the Texas Educational Agency. *Calor* is her first book (WRS).

Rudolfo A. Anaya (Rudolfo Alfonso Anaya)

Author

Anaya was born in 1937 in Pastura, New Mexico, and grew up in Santa Rosa and Albuquerque. A pioneer of Mexican-American literature, he has been writing for more than 30 years. His novel *Bless Me, Ultima* is a classic of Chicano literature.

Anaya's writings include fiction and nonfiction for children and adults. Among his recent works is a mystery series featuring Chicano detective Sonny Baca. Other fiction titles by the prolific Anaya include *Tortuga, Heart of Aztlán, The Silence of the Llano, Maya's Children, and My Land Sings*.

A strong proponent of Latino literature, Anaya speaks to educators about the importance of literature that accurately represents the cultures of Mexican Americans and Native Americans. Professor Emeritus at the University of New Mexico, he lives and writes in Albuquerque, New Mexico.

        \<http://www.unm.edu/~wrtgsw/anaya.html\>
        \<http://web.nmsu.edu/~tomlynch/swlit.anaya.html\>
        \<http://www.sdcoe.k12.ca.us/score/rona/author.html\>

George Ancona (Jorge Efrain Ancona)

Author and illustrator

George Ancona was born in 1929 in New York and grew up in Brooklyn. His parents were from Mexico, and George spoke Spanish before he learned English. As a teenager he worked as an auto mechanic and carpenter, and made money collecting scrap paper and junk to sell. After high school graduation he went to Mexico to get to know his grandparents and other family, and spent six months painting at the Academy of San Carlos in Mexico, where he met Rufino Tamayo, José Clemente Orozco, Diego Rivera, and Frida Kahlo.

When he returned to New York, he married, started a family, and worked as a graphic designer. Ten years later he began work as a professional photographer. This award-winning author and illustrator lives with his wife and some of his six children in Santa Fe, New Mexico (*Something*, vol. 85).

        \<http://teacher.scholastic.com/authorsandbooks/authors/ancona/bio.htm\>
        \<http://www.eduplace.com/kids/hmr/mtai/ancona.html\>

Gloria Anzaldúa (Gloria Evanjelina Anzaldúa)

Author

Anzaldúa was born in 1942 in south Texas into a family that had owned land since the eighteenth century. She attended Pan American University and the University of Texas at Austin and earned a Ph.D. from the University of California at Santa Cruz. She worked as a teacher in Texas and as a lecturer at Norwich University, Georgetown University, Colorado University, San Francisco State University, and the University of California.

She is the author of *Borderlands/La Frontera*, editor of *Making Face, Making Soul*, and co-editor of *This Bridge Called My Back*. Her works are included in many anthologies. *Borderlands* was voted one of the 100 best books of the 20th century by *Utne Reader* and *Hungry Mind Review*. She received an American Book Award in 1986 for *This Bridge Called My Back*. Anzaldúa now lives and writes in Santa Cruz, California.

<http://www.mankato.msus.edu/depts/worldsot/anza.htm>

Jeanne Arnold

Illustrator

Jeanne Arnold, a freelance illustrator and painter, attended Johnson State College in Vermont and studied art at the International School of Art in Umbria, Italy. Illustrator of the five *Carlos* books by Jan Romero Stevens, Arnold was inspired by Latin American folk artists, the Mexican painter Diego Rivera, and painters in Taos, New Mexico. Arnold lives with her husband in Salt Lake City, Utah. She enjoys hiking, gardening, skiing, and backpacking in the desert.

Ana Baca

Author and illustrator

Ana Baca is a native of New Mexico. She earned degrees in English literature from Stanford University and the University of New Mexico. Her first picture book, *Benito's Bizcochitos*, is based on her grandmother's recipe for bizcochitos, traditional Christmas cookies. Baca now lives and works in Albuquerque, New Mexico.

Alejandra Balestra

Translator

Alejandra Balestra, translator of *Pepita Takes Time* into Spanish, is originally from Argentina. She immigrated to the United States in the 1980s. Balestra is coordinator of the "Recovering the U.S. Hispanic Literary Heritage" project at Arte Público Press in Houston, Texas.

<http://www.arte.uh.edu/Arte_Publico_Press/arte_publico_press.html>

Diane Gonzales Bertrand

Author

Diane Gonzales Bertrand is a teacher and writer from San Antonio, Texas. Diane had six brothers and sisters, and wrote her first novel when she was in fifth grade! Bertrand attended college in San Antonio and taught high school English for seven years. Her *Close to the Heart*, *Carousel of Dreams*, and *Touchdown for Love* were the first romance novels to feature Mexican Americans as main characters. Bertrand's titles for children and young adults include *Sweet Fifteen*, *Trino's Choice*, *Trino's Time*, *Alicia's Treasure*, and *Lessons of the Game*. This author and teacher is happy that her works give readers a feeling of pride in their customs and traditions.

Bertrand is now Writer-in-Residence at St. Mary's University in San Antonio. She lives with her husband and their children, Nicky and Suzanne. (*Something*, vol. 106)
<http://www.childrenslit.com/f_dianegonzales.html>

Osvaldo J. Blanco

Translator

Osvaldo Blanco was born in Argentina. When he was 19, his novella was published in an anthology of Latin American, American, and English writers. He came to the United States in 1962, and lives and works in New York. Blanco has translated a dozen books, including mysteries, westerns, and science fiction. He has written and adapted literary works for radio and television. He is a co-author of *Green Force Five*, an ecological adventure strip that has been published in several languages in more than 50 newspapers worldwide. Mr. Blanco continues to write and translate, teaches English to Spanish literary translation at New York University, and contributes to journals of translator's associations in the United States and in Latin America (Blanco).

Isabel Campoy

Translator

F. Isabel Campoy translated *Qué montón de tamales!* by Gary Soto, *La casa adormecida* by Audrey Wood, *Growing Vegetable Soup* and *Feathers for Lunch* by Lois Ehlert, and *Hop Jump* by Ellen Stoll Walsh. She and Alma Flor Ada participated in the Authors in the Class Institute developed by the Bilingual Education/Language Academy of the San Francisco Unified School District. She is a member of the board of directors of the Friends & Foundation of the San Francisco Public Library.

Yanitzia Canetti

Translator and author

Yanitzia Canetti has translated more than 100 books! In addition she is the author of more than 30 books, including *Carlito Ropes the Twister*, *Al otro lado*, *Las babuchas de la mala suerte*, and *The Mural*. She has written articles for periodicals in Cuba, Spain, Italy, Mexico, Puerto Rico, Venezuela, and the United States.

Canetti was born in Havana, Cuba, in 1967. She learned to read and write when she was four, and is fluent in Spanish, English, and Italian. She earned a bachelor's degree in journalism, a master's in linguistics, and a Ph.D. in literature. A professional photographer, Canetti's photography has been included in numerous international expositions, and her photographs are part of collections in art galleries in Denmark, Mexico, Spain, and Italy. Canetti now lives near Boston, where she works as an editor and translator.

<http://www.yanitziacanetti.com/>
<http://www.eduplace.com/kids/hml/autores/canetti.html> (in Spanish)

Julia Mercedes Castilla

Translator and author

Julia Mercedes Castilla translated *Benito's Bizcochitos, Magda's Tortillas*, and *Family, Familia*. She is the author of *Emilio*, a novel for young adults, and *Aventuras de un niño de la calle*, a novel in Spanish. Castilla was born in Colombia and has lived in the United States for more than 25 years. The mother of three grown children, she lives in Houston, Texas.

<http://www.scbwi-houston.org/Julia%20Castilla.htm>

Joe Cepeda

Iillustrator

Joe Cepeda lives in Rosemead, California, with his wife and son. Cepeda has illustrated a number of books, including *Nappy Hair, What a Truly Cool World, Flyers,* and *Gracias, the Thanksgiving Turkey.* He has illustrated three titles by Gary Soto: *Big Bushy Mustache, The Cat's Meow*, and *The Old Man and His Door*.

<http://www.eduplace.com/kids/hmr/mtai/cepeda.html>

Becky Chavarría-Cháirez

Author

Becky Chavarría-Cháirez grew up in San Antonio, Texas. She has been a radio commentator on the Dallas National Public Radio station. In 1993 she received the Vivian Castleberry Award for radio commentary. Her works have been published in newspapers, journals, and magazines. Chavarría-Cháirez lives with her husband and two daughters in Dallas, Texas. She owns Catchphrases PR, a public/media relations company specializing in cross-cultural communications. She is dedicated to helping others understand and appreciate her Mexican-American heritage.

<http://www.childrenslit.com/f_beckychavarria.html>

Robin Cherin

Illustrator

Robin Cherin is an artist and co-illustrator of *My Aunt Otilia's Spirits* by Richard García. She was production manager and designer for the first 20 books from Children's Book Press. From 1968 to 1993 Cherin worked in fine art, illustration, and design and commercial printing in San Francisco. Her experience includes working as a painter and printmaker. Recently she has been

working in mixed media and collage. She now lives in Berkeley, California, where she continues to work in the art field (Cherin).
<http://www.artmecca.com/artwork/RobinCherin.htm>

Sandra Cisneros

Author

Sandra Cisneros is originally from Chicago. She was born in 1954, the only girl in a family of six boys. Her mother was Mexican-American, and her father was Mexican. The family moved between Mexico City and Chicago. Sandra was shy and did not do well in school, but after her mother got her a library card, she started to read. In high school she began to get recognition for her writing. After graduating from high school, she attended Loyola University and the Iowa Writers' Workshop. She has taught at the University of California, the University of Michigan, the University of New Mexico, and California State University at Chico.

Titles by Cisneros include *The House on Mango Street, Woman Hollering Creek, Loose Woman*, and *My Wicked Wicked Ways* and her works are included in many anthologies. The recipient of numerous awards, Cisneros now lives in San Antonio, Texas.
<http://www.lasmujeres.com/sandracisneros/cisnerosbio.shtml>

Roberta Collier-Morales

Illustrator

Roberta Collier-Morales is an art teacher. She has worked as an illustrator for more than 18 years. She is working on her master's degree at Marywood College in Pennsylvania. The illustrator of *Salsa* by Lillian Colón-Vilá, she also has provided illustrations for a number of picture books, including Bible stories, books about fairies and unicorns, a book about death, and books about endangered species. She is the illustrator of Diane DeAnda's short story collection, *The Immortal Rooster and Other Stories*. The mother of two children, Christian and Kara, she lives in Boulder, Colorado.

Raul Colón

Illustrator

Raul Colón illustrated *Tomás and the Library Lady, A Band of Angels, Habibi, Buoy, Hercules, My Mamá Had a Dancing Heart, A Weave of Words, Yolanda's Genius*, and others. His work has appeared on book jackets and in magazines and newspapers. He earned a silver medal from the Society of Illustrators for the illustrations in *Always My Dad*, his first children's book.

He illustrated the 1999 Texas Reading Club manual and related materials, and was a speaker at the 1999 Texas Library Association annual conference. The "Literacy Begins at Home" poster and bookmark taken from *Tomás and the Library Lady* are a part of the American Library Association's graphics catalog. Colón is also the creator of the 2000 National Children's Book Week streamers from the Children's Book Council. His works have appeared in *New York Times Book Review, Redbook*, and *Smithsonian*. Colón has lived in Florida and Puerto Rico, but now lives in New York.
<http://www.randomhouse.com/catalog/display.pperl?isbn=0385325398#bio>

Lillian Colón-Vilá

Author

Lillian Colón-Vilá is a bilingual education teacher in Oldsmar, Florida. She earned her B.A. in English literature from the University of Puerto Rico and her M.A. in Latin American and Caribbean Studies from New York University. Colón-Vilá shares her love for literature and art by developing after-school programs for children. She has also conducted workshops for teachers. In all her work, she connects literature, drama, dance, and art. *Salsa* is her first book. She lives in Tarpon Springs, Florida.

Claire B. Cotts

Illustrator

Claire B. Cotts illustrated *Manuela's Gift* by Kristyn Rehling Estes and *The Christmas Gift* by Francisco Jiménez. Her paintings have appeared in many galleries and museums in California. Cotts has lived in Turkey, Mexico, and Italy. She now lives in Berkeley, California, with her cat named Cowboy.

Patricia Hinton Davison

Translator

Patricia Davison was born in Monterrey, Mexico. She earned a B.A. degree at Centro Internacional de Capacitacion e Idiomas and an M.A. degree from the University of the Americas in Cholula, Puebla, Mexico. She is a professor in the Modern Languages Department of Northern Arizona University in Flagstaff, Arizona. Davison is also the Director and Program Coordinator of the Spanish Immersion Program at the University. Her areas of specialization are Spanish language and bilingual proficiency certification.

Alex Pardo DeLange

Illustrator

Alex Pardo DeLange was born in Venezuela, and educated in Argentina and the United States. She graduated from the University of Miami with a degree in fine arts and began her artistic career as a freelancer for advertising and design agencies. She has illustrated the *Pepita* books, *Sip, Slurp, Soup, Soup*, and *My Family Circus* by Mary Dixon Lake. She lives with her husband and three children in Florida.

María Isabel Delgado

Author

Isabel Delgado is a native of Brownsville, Texas. She earned a degree in education from the University of Houston. Delgado is a bilingual teacher in Grand Prairie, Texas. She was named

Teacher of the Year in Grand Prairie in 1993. *Chave's Memories,* her first book, is based on her memories of growing up on the border. Delgado now lives in Arlington, Texas.

Lidia Díaz

Translator

Originally from Buenos Aires, Argentina, Díaz is the first of her family to finish high school and graduate from a university. In 1988 with her husband and two children, she moved to Pennsylvania, earned a Ph.D. degree, and taught at Penn State University. Since 1996 she has worked at the University of Texas at Brownsville. Díaz is active in her field, presenting papers at conferences, and publishing articles and reviews. She is director of the university drama group and sponsor of the Cinema Club. A freelancer, her favorite translation works are in children's literature (Diaz).

<http://pubs.utb.edu/orange_white/fall1999/06heads.htm>

Arthur Dorros

Author and illustrator

Arthur Dorros was born in Washington, D.C. His father was a storyteller, and his mother was quick to provide Arthur art supplies. He attended the University of Wisconsin, where he earned a B.A. degree, and Pacific Oaks College, where he did postgraduate studies and earned teaching certification. He lived in South America for a year. His hobbies include carpentry, filmmaking, hiking, and horticulture, and he has worked as a builder and carpenter, teacher, photographer, and longshoreman.

The author and illustrator of a number of award-winning books in science and social studies, Dorros is fascinated by the richness of peoples with two cultures and languages. He lives in Seattle, Washington, with his wife and son. He enjoys visiting schools and working with children and encouraging them to do their own writing and illustrating (*Something*, vol. 78).

<http://falcon.jmu.edu/~ramseyil/dorros.htm>
<http://teacher.scholastic.com/authorsandbooks/authorvisit/dorros.htm>

Sandra Marulanda Dorros

Translator

Sandra Marulanda Dorros translated *Abuela*, *Radio Man*, and *La Isla*, which were written by her husband, Arthur Dorros. Mrs. Dorros grew up in Colombia, South America and came to the United States in 1980. She lives in Seattle with her husband and son, and teaches Spanish at the University of Washington.

Gaspar Enriquez

Illustrator

Gaspar Enriquez is a native of El Paso, Texas. He obtained a bachelor's degree from the University of Texas at El Paso and a master's degree from New Mexico State University. Enríquez is an art instructor at Bowie High School in El Paso.

His artwork earned him a Mid-America Arts Alliance Fellowship in 1994. His work was included in the *Chicano Art: Resistance and Affirmation* traveling show in the early 1990s. He considers his art a depiction of personal relationships and events of his bicultural life and environment, and a recording of Mexican-American lifestyles. He and his wife live in San Elizario, Texas, in a house that was built by his wife's great-great-grandfather.

<http://www.adairmargo.com/inventory/enriquez.asp

<http://www.cincopuntos.com/illustrator.ssd?name=Gaspar+Enriquez&s=2c388617a42f 4d23)>

D. H. Figueredo

Author

D. H. Figueredo was born in 1951 in Cuba. He has lived in New Jersey since he was a teenager. His picture book, *When This World Was New*, was inspired by his father's story of how he first walked on snow after coming to the United States from the Caribbean. Figueredo told the story to his son, who encouraged him to write the story. He did so, taking three years, and that picture book is the result. Figueredo is a librarian at Bloomfield College and a professor at Montclair State University. He lives with his family in Pistcataway, New Jersey (Figueredo).

<http://leeandlow.com/books/world.html>

Mary Sue Galindo

Author

Mary Sue Galindo is a writer and teacher. *Icy Watermelon*, her first picture book, was written because she saw a need for children's literature that represented her culture. As a child she enjoyed reading Nancy Drew mysteries and books by Laura Ingalls Wilder, but saw none of her personal experiences reflected in those works. Galindo was born in west Texas and grew up in Sonora, Texas, where schools were segregated until 1970 (Thomas).

Galindo has been a presenter at various conferences in Texas. She worked with El Cenizo Project-BRIDGE Literary Group, in which youth worked on an oral history, read and wrote poetry, and produced and distributed a community newsletter. She and her husband and three children live near Austin, Texas.

Daniel Galvez

Illustrator

Daniel Galvez attended the College of Arts and Crafts in Oakland and San Francisco State University, and received bachelor's and master's degrees in fine arts. Galvez has been painting murals since 1976. His murals include a memorial to veterans of the Vietnam War, a tribute to

Malcolm X, and a mural on Chinese immigration in California. He has been commissioned to paint murals for the Oakland/Alameda County Coliseum, the Alternative Museum in New York City, the San Francisco Art Institute, the California Arts Council, the Washington State Arts Commission, and the U.S. Department of the Interior. He lives in Oakland, California, with his wife Joan, a librarian. <http://www.ci.nyc.ny.us/html/dcla/html/panyc/galvez.html>
<http://www.sfmission.com/21murals/index.htm>
<http://www.hispanicvista.com/html/arts000905.html>

Geronimo Garcia

Illustrator

Geronimo Garcia was born and grew up in El Paso, Texas. His father was in the Navy and sent home comic books that he had drawn himself. Garcia decided that he wanted to be a commercial artist, attended the Art Institute of Houston, and eventually started his own company, Geronimooo Design.

He has illustrated three picture books for Cinco Puntos Press: *Tell Me a Cuento* by Joe Hayes, and *A Gift from Papá Diego* and *Grandma Fina and Her Wonderful Umbrellas* by Benjamin Alire Sáenz. For *A Gift from Papá Diego*, Garcia built figures from clay and painted them with acrylic paints. The clay figures were photographed to give the illustrations a three-dimensional effect.

Garcia is the designer of *An Elegy on the Death of César Chávez* that was illustrated by Gaspar Enriquez. He is the father of Adriana and Marina, and lives in El Paso, Texas.

Maria Garcia

Author

Maria Garcia, author of *The Adventures of Connie and Diego*, was born in 1944 in Kennedy, Texas. Her ancestry is Kiowa, Yaqui, Spanish, and French. The mother of six children, Garcia has lived and worked in San Jose and Oakland, California. She worked for the Comite de Mexico y Aztlán (COMEXAZ) and provided an educational research service about Chicanos and Mexicanos in California and the Southwest. Garcia believes that as human beings we should all be proud of who we are, a theme that is evident in her bilingual picture book, written years before the other titles in this guide.

Patricio García

Illustrator

Patricio García is a native of northern New Mexico. His specialties include family portraits and landscapes that express the Spanish culture of the area. Working mainly in pastels, García's works reflect family relationships and cultural traditions.

To illustrate *Los Ojos del tejedor/The Eyes of the Weaver*, García based his illustrations on actual characters and places depicted in the story. He created portraits of Cristina Ortega's grandfather and of Cristina as a child, and accurately pictured the Ortegas' looms and yarns and the village of Chimayó, New Mexico. The illustrations from *Los Ojos* were exhibited as a one-man show at the Governor's Gallery in Santa Fe, New Mexico. He now lives in Albuquerque, New Mexico, with his wife Mary.

Richard García (Richard Amado García)

Author

Richard García was born in San Francisco. His mother was Mexican-American and his father, Puerto Rican. He considered himself Mexican-American as he grew up, but now calls himself a "Mexi-Rican." García attended Warren Wilson College, where he earned a master's of fine arts degree.

His picture book, *My Aunt Otilia's Spirits*, was first published in 1978, long before most picture books featuring Puerto Rican characters. He is the author of *The Flying Garcías*. García's poetry has appeared in journals, including *The Américas Review*, *The Kenyon Review*, and *Parnassus*. His *Selected Poetry* was published in 1973. He earned a fellowship in poetry from the National Endowment for the Arts and a Pushcart Prize for poetry in 1997. He is now a poet-in-residence at the Children's Hospital in Los Angeles, California.

Stephanie Garcia

Illustrator

Stephanie Garcia illustrated *The Old Lady and the Birds* by Tony Johnson and *Snapshots from the Wedding* by Gary Soto. She won a Pura Belpré Award for Illustration in 1998 for her illustrations in *Snapshots from the Wedding*. She is also the artist of the cover of Melissa Wyatt's *When Jeff Comes Home* and *Swing Hammer Swing* by Jeff Torrington. Garcia's artwork illustrates a poster, available from the Children's Book Council, for National Hispanic Heritage Month.
<http://www.eduplace.com/kids/hmr/mtai/garcia.html>

Elizabeth Gómez (Elizabeth Gómez-Freer)

Illustrator

Elizabeth Gómez-Freer illustrated *The Upside Down Boy* by Juan Felipe Herrera. She is also illustrator of *A Movie in My Pillow* by Jorge Argueta. Originally from Mexico, she received a master's in fine arts degree from San Jose State University and a bachelor's degree from the San Francisco Art Institute. She has also studied in Mexico, Canada, and Italy.

Gomez-Freer's favorite art subjects are women, animals, and her personal history. Her art has been a part of numerous group and solo shows in California, Argentina, Canada, and Mexico. Influenced by the magic realism movement of Latin American artists and by Mexican popular art, she believes her art offers a way for her to understand and control her life. For *The Upside Down Boy*, Gómez created 15 original acrylic on paper paintings. This talented artist now lives in Cupertino, California.
<http://www.hexabus.com/art/Elizabeth/CurrentNews.html>
<http://www.sjsu.edu/depts/art_design/events/appliedmaterials/artists/artistf7.html>

Edward Gonzales

Illustrator

New Mexican Edward Gonzales illustrated *The Farolitos of Christmas* and *Farolitos for Abuelo*. As a child he read books from local public libraries and learned about art and art history. He earned a bachelor's degree in fine arts in 1971 from the University of New Mexico.

Gonzales is convinced that reading and achieving are directly related and that lack of education has dire consequences. A strong believer in literacy and reading, he has used his artistic talents to produce posters for schools and organizations, including the Tucson Public Schools, Literacy Volunteers of New Mexico, the New Mexico State Library, and the National Association for Chicana/Chicano Studies.

Through his paintings and artwork Gonzales seeks to portray Hispanic culture in a positive way. He frequently uses friends and relatives as models for illustrations. His biography and artwork are contained in a traveling exhibit called "Inspiring Young Minds to Dream." His art has been exhibited at the National Hispanic Cultural Center in Albuquerque, New Mexico. In 1998 he was named Hispanic Role Model of the Year.

Many of his paintings are available as calendars and posters. He lives in Rio Rancho, New Mexico, with his wife Susanna and their daughters Alicia and Selina.

<http://www.edwardgonzales.com/html/artist.html>
<http://www.redcrane.com/artbooks/spirit.htm>

Maya Christina González

Illustrator

Maya Christina González, a painter and graphic artist, was born in Lancaster, California. From the age of four, she wanted to draw people who looked like her. Christina was not taught Spanish at home and is still trying to learn that language. The family moved to Oregon when she was thirteen. Although she initially wanted to become a writer, when she was attending the University of Oregon, she took an art history class, dropped her writing classes, and switched to art.

González lives in San Francisco. Her art hangs in galleries and private homes, and has appeared in *Latina* and *People en Español* magazines. She has been a part of the Children's Book Press Outreach Program in schools in San Francisco and Los Angeles since 1996 (*Something*, vol. 115).

<http://www.mayagonzalez.com>

Jesús Guerrero Rea

Translator

Jesús Guerrero Rea translated *My Aunt Otilia's Spirits* by Richard García. With Harriet Rohmer he has adapted these titles: *Atariba & Niguayona, Cuna Song, Land of the Icy Death*, and *The Treasure of Guatavita* for Children's Book Press.

Susan Guevara

Illustrator

Susan Guevara was born in Walnut Creek, California. She graduated from the San Francisco Art Academy and studied at the Royal Academy of Fine Art in Belgium. Her first published illustrations were in 1990 in the picture book *Emmett's Snowball* by Ned Miller. In the years since, she has illustrated a number of picture books.

Her illustrations for *Chato's Kitchen* won the Pura Belpré award. When she is working on a book, Guevara does a great deal of research to find out about when and where the story happens. For *Chato's Kitchen*, she was inspired by Tijuana black velvet paintings. Guevara lives in Soda Springs, California, with her husband (*Something*, vol. 97).

Juan Felipe Herrera

Author

Juan Felipe Herrera is the son of migrant workers, a poet, an actor, a musician, and a teacher. He was born in California, and earned college degrees from Stanford University and from the University of California at Los Angeles. Herrera is a professor at California State University at Fresno, where he lives with his family and teaches Chicano and Latin American Studies.

<http://www.corona.bell.k12.ca.us/comm/juan.html>
<http://www.teacheruniverse.com/tools/language_corner/crash_boom_0401.htm>

Pilar Herrera

Translator

Pilar Herrera translated *Grandma Fina and Her Wonderful Umbrellas*. She is the Parental Engagement Coordinator of the El Paso Collaborative for Academic Excellence in the Education Department at the University of Texas at El Paso. The El Paso Collaborative is a coalition dedicated to education reform. Its members include school superintendents, college and university presidents, Chamber of Commerce heads, and the mayor. Herrera facilitates communication between schools and parents.

Pauline Rodriguez Howard

Illustrator

Pauline Rodriguez Howard is an artist and a native Texan of Spanish and Polish ancestry. Howard earned a bachelor's of fine arts degree from the University of Houston and attended the Glassell School of Art. A member of the Central Texas Pastel Society, she is known for her paintings as well as her book illustrations.

This illustrator believes that it is important not to present stereotypes. She frequently uses friends and family members as models for characters in her picture books. Howard lives in San Antonio, Texas, with her husband and two daughters.

Francisco Jiménez

Author

Francisco Jiménez was born in 1943 in San Pedro, Tlaquepaque, Mexico. In 1947 he and his family emigrated from Tlaquepaque to California, where they worked in the fields. He earned a Ph.D. degree from Columbia University and has taught at California State University, San Diego State University, Stanford University, University of Texas, Harvard, University of Notre Dame, and Wellesley College.

Jiménez has received a Woodrow Wilson fellowship, Ford Foundation grant, Outstanding Young Man of America award, Distinguished Leadership in Education award, and others. *The Circuit*, an autobiographical account of his childhood, won the Américas award, the Jane Addams Children's Award Honor Book, the Beatty Award, and the *Boston Globe-Horn Book* Award. Jiménez is Chairman of the Modern Languages and Literatures Department at Santa Clara University in Santa Clara, California, where he lives with his wife and three children (*Something*, vol. 108).

<http://www.scu.edu/SCU/Programs/Diversity/panch.html>

Elisa Kleven (Elisa Kleven Schneider)

Author and illustrator

Elisa Kleven is a writer and an artist. She was born in Los Angeles. Her father was a doctor and her mother, an artist. Although she did not study art, her mother, a printmaker, and her grandmother, a sculptor, encouraged her art and creative storytelling. Kleven grew up in Los Angeles and earned a degree in English from the University of California at Berkeley.

She has taught nursery school, fourth grade, and art, as well as being a weaver and toy maker. Under the name Elisa Schneider, she has published *The Merry-Go-Round Dog, Ernst, The Lion and the Little Red Bird*, and *The Paper Princess*. She published her first picture book in 1988, and has illustrated her own books and those written by other authors.

Kleven lives with her husband, Paul, daughter, Mia, and son, Ben, in Albany, California. She says that her children and her dog and cat inspire her books, and through her books, she hopes to inspire others to imagine and to play (*Something*, vol. 76).

<http://www.elisakleven.com/aboutelisa.html>
<http://dcn.davis.ca.us/~gizmo/1999/kleven.html>
<http://www.penguinputnam.com/Author/AuthorFrame/0,1018,,00.html?0000014333>

Ofelia Dumas Lachtman

Author

Ofelia Dumas Lachtman was born in Los Angeles to Mexican immigrant parents. She grew up in Los Angeles and attended Los Angeles City College and the University of California at Los Angeles. Lachtman's writings have been published in numerous newspapers and periodicals. In addition to the *Pepita* picture books, she has written an adult novel, *A Shell for Angela*, and several titles for younger readers. The mother of a grown son and daughter, Lachtman lives in Los Angeles.

<http://www.childrenslit.com/f_ofelialachtman.html>
<http://www.eduplace.com/kids/hmr/mtai/lachtman.html>

Cecily Lang

Illustrator

Cecily Lang was born in New York City. She earned a degree from San Francisco State University. Lang worked in Los Angeles in the animation industry before returning to New York. She has illustrated *A Birthday Basket for Tía* and *Pablo's Tree* by Pat Mora, and *Annie's Shabbat* by Sarah Marwil Lamstein. Lang's illustrations have appeared in magazines and textbooks. She makes her home in New York City with her husband and son.

Carmen Lomas Garza

Author and illustrator

Carmen Lomas Garza was born in Kingsville, Texas, in 1948. Her mother was a self-taught artist, and her father was a sheet metal and wood craftsman. Lomas Garza has warm memories of childhood in her family but unhappy memories of discrimination and being punished for speaking Spanish at school.

Lomas Garza has two art education degrees and a studio art degree. In 1995 she was the first Mexican-American artist to have a solo exhibition at the Hirshhorn Museum and Sculpture Garden in Washington, D.C. Her artwork has been exhibited in California, Texas, and New York. She is included in the anthology *Here Is My Kingdom*, and her art is on the cover of the *Pieces of the Heart* anthology. The Census 2000 poster features Lomas Garza's painting "Beds for Dreams/ Camas para sueños." She was a consultant for the 1997 movie *Selina*. Lomas Garza lives in San Francisco with her husband, Jerry Avila Carpenter, to whom she dedicates *Magic Windows*.
<http://mati.eas.asu.edu:8421/ChicanArte/html_pages/CarmenIssOutl.html>
<http://thecity.sfsu.edu/~galeria/clg_bio.html>

Loretta Lopez

Author and illustrator

Loretta Lopez was born in El Paso, Texas, and earned a degree in fine arts from Pratt Institute in Brooklyn, New York. López says she wanted to be an author and illustrator of children's books since she read *Bambi* in the third grade. Her older brothers and sisters gave her books as gifts for Christmas and birthdays.

According to Lopez, the first book that she read relating to Mexican-American culture was *And Now Miguel*. She identified with the food, language, traditions, and culture in that book. *The Birthday Swap* is based on a story and tradition from her family history. She also wrote *Say Hola to Spanish*, which was a Children's Book-of-the-Month Club selection, and two other titles in the *Say Hola* series.
<http://leeandlow.com/booktalk/lopez.html>

Ed Martínez

Illustrator

Ed Martínez illustrated *Tonio's Cat* by Mary Calhoun, *Three Kings' Day* by Lori Marie Carlson, *María de Sautuola* by Dennis Fradin, *My Prairie Summer* by Sarah Glasscock, and *Too Many Tamales* by Gary Soto. He was born in 1954 in Buenos Aires, Argentina. He enjoys painting landscapes and restoring an 18th century farmhouse. His wife, Deborah L. Chabrian, is also an artist. Martínez and his wife live in South Kent, Connecticut, with their son Oliver.
<http://www.eduplace.com/kids/hmr/mtai/martinez.html>

Consuelo Méndez (Consuelo Méndez Castillo)

Illustrator

Consuelo Méndez is from Caracas, Venezuela. She grew up in south Texas and studied art in San Francisco. She was a member of Mujeres Muralistas, a group of women artists in San Francisco. Her illustrations have appeared in two picture books: *Friends from the Other Side* by Gloria Anzaldúa and *Atariba & Niguayona*, which was adapted by Harriet Rohmer and Jesús Guerrero Rea. She now lives in San Francisco, California.

Teresa Mlawer

Translator

Teresa Mlawer is the president of Lectorum Publications. She was born in Havana, Cuba, and received her education in Cuba and the United States. This translator of more than 200 children's books has given lectures in Latin America, Spain, and the United States about the Spanish book market in the United States. Mlawer has conducted workshops to teach teachers about using children's books in Spanish in classroom teaching. Before becoming president of Lectorum in 1976, she worked in editing and sales at Macmillan and Simon & Schuster, and was Vice President in charge of domestic and international sales at Regents Publishing (Sarfatti).

Malaquias Montoya

Illustrator

Malaquias Montoya was born in 1938 in Albuquerque, New Mexico. His parents did not read or write Spanish or English, and the family worked as farmworkers to survive. After his parents divorced, his mother worked in the fields so that her children could obtain an education. Montoya remembers learning to draw on paper trays used to hold drying grapes in the San Joaquin Valley. He graduated from the University of California, Berkeley. Montoya has been an artist-in-residence, a visiting lecturer and professor, and has taught at community colleges in the San Francisco Bay Area. His art has been exhibited in Europe, Latin America, and the United States. He is a professor of art at the University of California, Davis.
<http://cougar.ucdavis.edu/chi/Montoya.html>

Pat Mora (Patricia Mora)

Author

The author of numerous books of poetry, essays, picture books, and an autobiography, Pat Mora was born in 1942 in El Paso, Texas. She attended Texas Western College and the University of Texas at El Paso. Mora loves poetry, and believes she is lucky because she grew up in a bilingual home and can speak and write in two languages.

Winner of a Southwest Book Award for two poetry books, she has been the recipient of numerous awards. Her initiative Día de los niños/Día de los libros is celebrated on April 30. The mother of three grown children, she divides her time between Kentucky and New Mexico, and keeps busy writing, speaking, and advocating reading (*Something*, vol. 92).

<http://www.patmora.com/> <http://voices.cla.umn.edu/authors/patmora.html>
<http://www.accd.edu/sac/english/portales/mora.htm>
<http://teacher.scholastic.com/authorsandbooks/authors/mora/tscript.htm>
<http://www.leeandlow.com/booktalk/mora.html>

Carmen Santiago Nodar

Author

Carmen Santiago Nodar grew up in the Bronx and Rockaway, New York. Her Puerto Rican parents spoke no English when they arrived in New York. As the oldest of nine children, she never owned a book nor had a book read to her during her childhood. She was forced to leave high school when she was a junior because of family poverty. She later completed her education, graduated from business school, and took college classes in literature and writing.

To make up for her childhood lack of books, she provided books, book clubs, and library visits for her children. Although her two grown children no longer live at home, Nodar continues to visit libraries and bookstores, and to read children's literature in Naples, Florida, where she lives with her husband (Nodar).

Cristina Ortega

Author

A writer and teacher, Ortega has taught first grade in Albuquerque for more than sixteen years. She has made a commitment to use her skills to help children appreciate their cultural identity. Cristina Ortega is a member of a family of weavers from Chimayó, New Mexico. Her book tells of the passing of the tradition of weaving from generation to generation since the early 1700s, when Gabriel Ortega settled in the north Río Grande Valley in what was then New Spain. Three hundred years later the weaving business is now in its eighth generation. Citizens in Chimayó remember Cristina, her parents, her grandfather, and his wonderful garden near the plaza where he grew vegetables and his own tobacco.

Diane Paterson

Illustrator

Diane Paterson grew up in a brownstone house in Brooklyn, New York. Her parents and grandparents nourished her artistic talent by giving young Diane pencils, crayons, paper, and coloring books, and teaching her to draw. She drew pictures of cats, pigeons, and even a picture of herself as a mother and artist sailing in a boat. Fulfilling her own prophecy, Paterson is now a mother and an artist married to a sailor and magician. She and her family live on the Gulf Coast of Florida (Paterson).

Amado M. Peña, Jr. (Amado Maurilio Peña, Jr.)

Illustrator

Artist Amado Peña was born in Kingsville, Texas. His father was a fireman, his mother was a homemaker and seamstress, and his sister Irene became a teacher. He graduated from Texas A & I University and worked as an art teacher in Texas for 16 years before becoming a full-time artist. Peña considers himself a mestizo of Hispanic and Yaqui Indian ancestry, and through his art he explores his heritage and cultures.

Because of their belief in the importance of education, Peña and his wife have established the Art Has Heart Foundation, which provides scholarships and grants to students in five southwestern states, and the Peña-Pascua Yaqui endowment for scholarships to members of the Pascua Yaqui Tribe of Arizona. Peña now lives on a ranch north of Santa Fe with his wife, J.B., who is a weaver. He works in his studio in Santa Fe, New Mexico, when he isn't traveling to shows and festivals around the country.

<http://www.penaofficial.com/bio.html>

Amada Irma Pérez

Amada Irma Pérez is a bilingual teacher in Oxnard, California. She immigrated from Mexico as a young child. She was one of six children, and her father worked in the fields. The story of *My Very Own Room* is Amada Irma's own story from her childhood.

Pérez has taught for 24 years, working with students from kindergarten to college-age adults. She considers herself a learner as well as a teacher and believes that education can transform lives in a positive way. Mrs. Pérez lives with her husband and two sons in Ventura County, California.

<http://equity4.clmer.csulb.edu/netshare/cti/cti_personal_profiles/perez.html>

Amy Prince

Translator

Amy Diane Prince is a translator. She translated *Benita/Benita Galeana* for Latin American Literary Review Press and *Tomás y la señora de la biblioteca* by Pat Mora.

Roger I. Reyes

Illustrator

A graphic artist and designer, Roger I. Reyes illustrated three books from Children's Book Press: *My Aunt Otilia's Spirits* by Richard García, and *The Little Horse of Seven Colors* and *Skyworld Woman*, both adapted by Harriet Rohmer and Mary Anchondo. He was born in Chicago of Filipino parentage. Reyes is now deceased (Lindeman).

Luis J. Rodríguez

Author

Luis J. Rodríguez has written poetry, an autobiography, and picture books. Born in Texas in 1954, Rodríguez grew up in Los Angeles. His writings about his involvement with gangs in *Always Running: La Vida Loca* earned a Carl Sandburg Award. He is active in working to prevent violence in Chicago, Los Angeles, and across the country. He founded Tía Chucha Press, which he named for his aunt. Rodríguez has received several literary and artistic awards, including a Lannan fellowship for poetry and a Chicago Artists Abroad grant. Rodríguez lives in Los Angeles with his wife Trini and their two sons.

<http://www.curbstone.org/authdetail.cfm?AuthID=10>
<http://www.poetrysociety.org/rodriguez.html>

Harriet Rohmer

Harriet Rohmer is the publisher and executive director of Children's Book Press. She was born in 1938 in Washington, D.C. Her interest in folktales of Latin America began when her son was in a Head Start program in San Francisco. Many of the students were Spanish speakers, but there were no books that represented their cultures. Rohmer founded Children's Book Press in San Francisco in 1975. At that time there were almost no children's books containing non-Anglo characters, and her purpose was to publish books that celebrate and honor diversity. She has edited and adapted more than 20 titles. The nonprofit Children's Book Press continues to provide quality multicultural books and literary outreach through the LitLinks program (*Something*, vol. 56).

<http://www.cbookpress.org/about.html>

Sylvia Rosa-Casanova

Author

Sylvia Rosa-Casanova was born and grew up in New York City. She had a grandmother just like Lucy's grandmother in *Mama Provi and the Pot of Rice*. *Mama Provi* is her first picture book. She lives in Congers, New York, with her husband, George, and their sons, Maxx and Nick.

Robert Roth

Illustrator

Roth grew up in Cold Spring Harbor, New York, and graduated from the Rhode Island School of Design with a fine arts degree. He has illustrated numerous picture books. Roth has received several honors, including an original art award from the Society of Illustrators. He lives in Massachusetts with his wife, Cheryl, and daughter, Cassidy.

Benjamin Alire Sáenz

Author

Benjamin Alire Sáenz was born in the village of Picacho, New Mexico, in his grandmother's house. Sáenz grew up speaking Spanish and English, considered being either an artist or a writer, and still enjoys creating art. His novels include *Carry Me Like Water* and *The House of Forgetting,* which will be made into a motion picture. His poetry titles are *Dark and Perfect Angels* and *Calendar of Dust*, which won the American Book Award. He has also published *Flowers from the Broken*, a book of short stories. An acclaimed poet, novelist, and short story writer, Sáenz is a professor at the University of Texas at El Paso.

<http://sparta.rice.edu/~erinm/Saenz.html#about>

<http://www.cincopuntos.com/papadieg.html>

Enrique O. Sánchez

Illustrator

Enrique O. Sánchez, a native of the Dominican Republic, has illustrated 12 books, including *Amelia's Road, A Is for the Americas, Speak English for Us, Marisol!*, and *Palampam Day*. Other titles he illustrated are *The Golden Flower* by Nina Jaffe, *María Molina and the Days of the Dead* by Kathleen Krull, *Big Enough* by Ofelia Dumas Lachtman, *Confetti* by Pat Mora, and *Lupe & Me* by Elizabeth Spurr. Sánchez and his wife Joan, also an artist, divide their time between Bar Harbor, Maine, and Miami, Florida.

Elizabeth Sayles

Illustrator

Elizabeth Sayles works as an illustrator and designer and teaches at the School of Visual Arts in New York City. In addition to *The Rainbow Tulip*, she has illustrated a number of books, including *Albie the Lifeguard, Five Little Kittens, This Mess, Outrageously Alice, The Little Black Truck*, and several others. Sayles lives with her husband and daughter in Valley Cottage, New York.

<http://houghtonmifflinbooks.com/catalog/authordetail.cfm?authorID=2676>

David Schecter

Writer

David Schecter is an editor and director of outreach programs at Children's Book Press. Books he has edited for Children's Book Press include *In My Family* and *Magic Windows* by Carmen Lomas Garza. He co-wrote *The Woman Who Outshone the Sun* with Rosalma Zubizarreta and Harriet Rohmer. Schecter lives in San Francisco.

Simón Silva

Illustrator

Simón Silva was born in Mexicalli, Mexico in 1961. One of 11 children, he grew up in Holtville, California. He started working in the fields when he was eight years old. He and his family traveled to Washington and Oregon looking for work. Because of his family's lack of educational support and the necessity of working in the fields, Silva grew up with low self-esteem and without respect for his cultural background. Through art he found his purpose in life, pursued an education, and learned to appreciate his culture. He earned a degree in fine arts from the Art Center College of Design in Pasadena, California.

Silva lectures at schools around the country, sharing his experiences and art and the idea that bilingualism and biculturalism are assets. His awareness of the richness of his heritage inspires his art, and he takes pride in being a part of the mixture of nationalities that have made this country great. Silva lives with his wife, María, and their two sons in San Bernardino, California.

<http://www.silvasimon.com/bio.htm>

Elly Simmons

Illustrator

Elly Simmons was born in New York City and grew up in San Francisco. She established a studio in West Marin County in 1975 and graduated from San Jose State University in 1978. This internationally exhibited artist uses her art to express her feelings about injustice and to celebrate the beauty of life. Her artwork has gained Simmons many awards. Simmons and her family live in Lagunitas, California. She is married to an energy conservation consultant, and has one daughter, Maralisa (Simmons).

<http://www.ellysimmons.com>

Gary Soto

Author

Gary Soto, a well-known writer of poetry, fiction, and nonfiction, was born in 1952 in Fresno, California. His family did not have books in their home, and no one encouraged Gary to read. After finding a collection of poems, *The New American Poetry*, he was inspired to start writing poetry. He earned a degree in English at California State University and a Masters of Fine Arts in Creative Writing from the University of California at Irvine.

A prolific writer, Soto has received a number of prestigious awards for his writings, including an American Book Award, Beatty Award, Carnegie Medal, Reading Magic Award, and a Guggenheim fellowship. In his "spare" time, Soto is a volunteer English teacher at his church. He lives with his wife, Carolyn, their daughter, Mariko, and their cats, Corky and Sharkie, in Berkeley, California (*Something*, vol. 80).

<http://www.garysoto.com/>
<http://www.edupaperback.org/authorbios/Soto_Gary.html>

Jan Romero Stevens

Author

Jan Romero Stevens was born in 1953 in Las Vegas, New Mexico, and died on February 21, 2000. She lived in Flagstaff, Arizona, with her husband, Fred, and her two sons, Jacob and Paul. In addition to her picture books, she wrote for newspapers and magazines for 18 years and played in a local orchestra.

The response of children in Arizona to the first *Carlos* book encouraged her to continue the series. During her lifetime she received many awards (*Something*, vol. 95). A scholarship fund has been established in her memory at Northern Arizona University in Flagstaff ("Jan").

Yvonne Symank

Illustrator

Yvonne Symank is a freelance artist who specializes in designs for children. She graduated from the University of Houston. Symank has designed many cards, books, and products for children. Symank lives in Katy, Texas. She illustrated *Chave's Memories* by Isabel Delgado.

Jane Tenorio-Coscarelli

Author and illustrator

Jane Tenorio-Coscarelli is an author, illustrator, designer, and speaker. A freelance artist who loves quilting, she owns her own company, Quarter Inch Designs & Publishing, in Murrieta, California. She has appeared on "Simply Quilts," an HGTV television program, and as a stunt quilter in the movie "How to Make an American Quilt."

Her fascination with quilts is apparent in her picture books, *The Piñata Quilt, The Tamale Quilt,* and *The Tortilla Quilt*. Tenorio-Coscarelli wrote and illustrated these books, which include traditions, stories, patterns, and recipes. She is available for school assemblies and classroom lectures to educate children about quilting, Hispanic culture, and book publishing. She also offers quilting workshops and classes and is available for luncheon speaking engagements. In her "free" time, she enjoys drawing, cooking, listening to music, and spending time with her husband, Bill, and their children, Nicole and Dominic.

<http://www.quarterinchpublishing.com>

Leyla Torres

Author and illustrator

Leyla Torres was born in 1960 in Bogota, Colombia. She earned a degree in fine arts and education, worked as an artist, and taught art in Bogota. When she came to the United States, she planned to stay for one year. She has worked as a translator, interpreter, teacher, and photographer. Her art has been shown in solo and group exhibits in Colombia and in the United States.

In addition to *Liliana's Grandmothers/Las abuelas de Liliana*, Torres has written and illustrated *Subway Sparrow/Gorrión del metro* and *Saturday Sancocho/El sancocho del sábado*. Torres lives with her husband in New York and Vermont.

<http://www.eduplace.com/kids/hmr/mtai/torres.html>

Liliana Valenzuela

Translator

Liliana Valenzuela, translator of *Hairs/Pelitos*, is a writer and anthropologist. Valenzuela came to the United States from Mexico City in 1981. She earned two degrees in literature and the Premio Literario Chicano from the University of California at Irvine in 1989.

After she had her first child, she began to translate business documents. She met Sandra Cisneros in Austin, Texas, before Cisneros moved to San Antonio. Valenzuela volunteered to translate one of Cisneros' short stories and eventually translated several of Cisneros' works. She enjoys the challenges of literary translating, and advises would-be translators to make a commitment and put their best effort behind it. She lives in Austin, Texas.

<http://www.aatia.org/readroom/Interviw.htm>

Carlos Vázquez

Illustrator

Carlos Vázquez illustrated *América Is Her Name*. He was born in Mexico. His fields of study in Mexico were physics and art. Vázquez now teaches in bilingual adult education in New York City. *América Is Her Name* is his first picture book.

Anne Vega

Illustrator

Anne Vega lives and works in Nashville, Tennessee, with her husband and two children. Her husband, Robert, is also an artist.

Vega attended the Columbus School of Art and Design in Ohio and the Academy of Art in San Francisco. *Magda's Tortillas* is her first picture book, and her illustrations have appeared on numerous book covers.

Eida de la Vega

Translator

Eida de la Vega was born in 1967 in Havana, Cuba. Her grandmother taught her to read when she was three years old, and her mother worked at the National Library, so Eida spent much of her early childhood in the library reading. She earned a degree in biochemistry from Havana University and worked in a lab before working at the National Library until 1995 when she came to the United States.

Vega enjoys translating books and believes translating is a way to say thank you to those who made it possible for her to read stories as a child. Because she is bilingual, she is able to do translations for income, taking advantage of the market created by the increasing number of Spanish speakers in this country. She and her husband and son, Eric, live in New Jersey (DelRisco).

Tino Villanueva

Translator and author

Tino Villanueva is a well-known poet and teacher. Originally from San Marcos, Texas, he was born in 1941. He attended universities in Texas and New York. He worked as a farm worker and an assembly-line worker, and served in the army before beginning his teaching career. In Boston he was Program Director for "La Hora Hispana" broadcast by Harvard University radio station WHRB. The recipient of an American Book Award in 1994, Villanueva has published several works of poetry. He has taught at Oxford and Harvard and is currently a professor at Boston University, where he is editor of *Imagine*, a Chicano poetry journal.

        \<http://www.bu.edu/mfll/fac/span/villanueva.html>
        \<http://www.library.swt.edu/swwc/archives/writers/villanueva.html>
        \<http://mati.eas.asu.edu:8421/bilingual/HTML/shaking.html>

Terry Ybáñez

Illustrator

Terry Ybáñez is a bilingual kindergarten teacher and artist in San Antonio, Texas. Books she has illustrated include *Hairs/Pelitos* and *The Christmas Tree/El árbol de Navidad*. Her artwork has been exhibited at the Guadalupe Cultural Arts Center in San Antonio, at the University of Mexico in Mexico City, and in San Francisco at the Galeria de la Raza.

Rosalma Zubizarreta

Translator

Rosalma (Rosa) Zubizarreta translated *Family Pictures*, *Something Is Growing*, *The Lizard and the Sun*, *Stories for the Telling*, and *The Malachite Palace*. She considers herself lucky to be able to express herself in two languages and to understand the world through both languages. She is the daughter of the multi-talented Alma Flor Ada.

Works Cited

Book jackets and author pages from picture books in Part II.
Library of Congress online catalog.
Web sites as indicated for each biographical entry.

Articles:

Figueredo, D.H. "How I Came to Write the Book." *Amazon.com* 20 April 1999.

"Jan Stevens, Journalist and Children's Author." *Arizona Sun Online* 22 Feb. 2000: n.pag.

Thomas, Sherry. "Heat Inspired Icy Watermelon." *HoustonChronicle.com* 02 Jan. 2001: n.pag.

Books:

Something About the Author. 121 vols. to date. Gale Research, 1971.

E-mail:

Blanco, Osvaldo. "Re: Bio information for book proposal." E-mail to Sherry York. 4 Dec. 2000.

Cherin, Robin. "Robin Cherin's Bio Info." E-mail to Sherry York. 18 June 2001.

DelRisco, Eida. "Re: Request for biographical info." E-mail to Sherry York. 25 Oct. 2000.

Diaz, Lidia. "Book translator?" E-mail to Sherry York. 15 Nov. 2000.

Lindeman, Susan. "Biographical info." E-mail to Sherry York. 20 June 2001.

Sarfatti, Esther. "Teresa Mlawer's bio." E-mail to Sherry York. 10 May 2001.

Unpublished:

Nodar, Carmen Santiago. "Author Information Sheets." Albert Whitman, n.d.

Paterson, Diane. "Author Information Sheet." Albert Whitman, 1997.

Simmons, Elly. "Elly Simmons." Press Kit. Lagunitas, California.

Web sites:

WRS Publishing Web site, no longer available.

For Further Reading

Authors & Artists for Young Adults. 38 vols. to date. Gale Research, 1989- .

Contemporary Authors. Gale Research, 1962, 1979- .

Day, Frances Ann. *Latina and Latino Voices in Literature*. Heinemann, 1997.

Dictionary of Literary Biography. Gale Research, 1978- .

Part *IV*

Subject–Title Index

T his section is provided for teachers and librarians who may need books on specific subjects. The index will also be useful for parents and students who are especially interested in certain subjects or books about a specific cultural group. Some subjects have been combined to avoid redundancy, and the term "juvenile" has been eliminated for the purposes of this list. Library of Congress subjects have been retained, although certain subjects, such as "Hispanic Americans," would seem to apply to almost every title in this guide. Complete Library of Congress subject headings are provided in Part II. As the reader browses through these subjects, certain gaps will be apparent. It is hoped that future picture books by Latinos will fill in the missing subjects so that every possible subject, theme, and concept will be addressed in a Latino-authored picture book.

Adoption—Fiction
Pablo's Tree

Agricultural workers—California
Calling the Doves/El canto de las palomas

American poetry
Angels Ride Bikes and Other Fall Poems/ Los Ángeles Andan en Bicicleta y otros poemas de otoño
From the Bellybutton of the Moon and Other Summer Poems/Del Ombligo de la Luna y otros poemas de verano
Laughing Tomatoes and Other Spring

Poems/Jitomates Risueños y otros poemas de primavera

Aunts—Fiction
My Aunt Otilia's Spirits/Los espíritus de mi Tía Otilia

Authors, American
Calling the Doves/El canto de las palomas

Autumn—Poetry
Angels Ride Bikes and Other Fall Poems/ Los Ángeles Andan en Bicicleta y otros poemas de otoño

Bedrooms—Fiction
My Very Own Room/Mi propio cuartito

Behavior—Fiction
Pepita Takes Time/Pepita, siempre tarde

Bilingualism—Fiction
Pepita Talks Twice/Pepita habla dos veces

Birds—Fiction
Gorrión del metro
Subway Sparrow

Birthdays—Fiction
A Birthday Basket for Tía
The Birthday Swap
Una canasta de cumpleaños para Tía
Chato and the Party Animals
A Gift from Papá Diego/Un regalo de Papá Diego
Grandma Fina and Her Wonderful Umbrellas/La Abuelita Fina y sus sombrillas maravillosas
Magda's Tortillas/Las tortillas de Magda
Pablo's Tree
The Piñata Quilt
¡Qué sorpresa de cumpleaños!

Books and reading—Fiction
Tomás and the Library Lady
Tomás y la señora de la biblioteca

Brothers and sisters—Fiction
The Adventures of Connie and Diego/ Los aventuras de Connie y Diego

California—Social life and customs
Calling the Doves/El canto de las palomas

Caribbean Area—Fiction
Isla
La isla

Cats—Fiction
A Birthday Basket for Tía
Una canasta de cumpleaños para Tía

Chato and the Party Animals
Chato y su cena
Chato's Kitchen

Chávez, César, 1927–1993—Poetry
An Elegy on the Death of César Chávez

Chickenpox—Fiction
Mama Provi and the Pot of Rice

Children of migrant laborers—California
Calling the Doves/El canto de las palomas

Children's poetry, American—Translations into Spanish
Angels Ride Bikes and Other Fall Poems/ Los Ángeles Andan en Bicicleta y otros poemas de otoño
An Elegy on the Death of César Chávez
From the Bellybutton of the Moon and Other Summer Poems/ Del Ombligo de la Luna y otros poemas de verano
Laughing Tomatoes and Other Spring Poems/Jitomates Risueños y otros poemas de primavera

Children's poetry, Hispanic American (Spanish)—Translations English/Spanish
Angels Ride Bikes and Other Fall Poems/ Los Ángeles Andan en Bicicleta y otros poemas de otoño
From the Bellybutton of the Moon and Other Summer Poems/Del Ombligo de la Luna y otros poemas de verano
Laughing Tomatoes and Other Spring Poems/Jitomates Risueños y otros poemas de primavera

Christmas—Fiction
Benito's Bizcochitos/Los bizcochitos de Benito
The Christmas Tree/El árbol de Navidad
Farolitos for Abuelo
The Farolitos of Christmas

Qué montón de tamales!
The Tamale Quilt
Too Many Tamales

Christmas trees—Fiction
The Christmas Tree/El árbol de Navidad

Cleanliness—Fiction
Carlos and the Squash Plant/Carlos y la planta de calabaza

Color—Fiction
Pepita Thinks Pink/Pepita y el color rosado

Cookery, Chinese—Fiction
Carlos Digs to China/Carlos excava hasta la China

Cookery, Mexican—Fiction
Magda's Tortillas/Las tortillas de Magda

Cookies—Fiction
Benito's Bizcochitos/Los bizcochitos de Benito

Corn—Fiction
Carlos and the Cornfield/Carlos y la milpa de maíz

Death—Fiction
Abuelita's Paradise
Farolitos for Abuelo
El Paraíso de Abuelita

Decision making—Fiction
Pepita Talks Twice/Pepita habla dos veces

Dogs—Fiction
Hooray! A Piñata!
Viva! Una piñata!

Emigration and immigration—Fiction
Un mundo nuevo
When This World Was New

Family
Calor: A Story of Warmth for All Ages

Family—California—Los Angeles—Poetry
Angels Ride Bikes and Other Fall Poems/Los Ángeles Andan en Bicicleta y otros poemas de otoño

Family life—Fiction
My Very Own Room/Mi propio cuartito
Sip, Slurp, Soup, Soup/Caldo, caldo, caldo

Family reunions—Fiction
Family, Familia

Farm life—Fiction
Carlos and the Squash Plant/Carlos y la planta de calabaza

Farm life—New Mexico—Fiction
Carlos and the Cornfield/Carlos y la milpa de maíz
Carlos and the Skunk/Carlos y el zorrillo

Fathers and sons—Fiction
Big Bushy Mustache
Un mundo nuevo
When This World Was New

Fear—Fiction
Un mundo nuevo
When This World Was New

Festivals
Fiesta U.S.A.

Festivals—United States
Fiesta U.S.A.

Flight—Fiction
Abuela

Food—Fiction
Mama Provi and the Pot of Rice

Friendship—Fiction
Friends from the Other Side/Amigos del otro lado
Pepita Thinks Pink/Pepita y el color rosado

Gangs—Fiction
> *It Doesn't Have To Be This Way/No tiene que ser así*

Gifts—Fiction
> *A Birthday Basket for Tía*
> *Una canasta de cumpleaños para Tía*

Grandfathers—Fiction
> *Farolitos for Abuelo*
> *The Farolitos of Christmas*
> *A Gift from Papá Diego/Un regalo de Papá Diego*
> *Los Ojos del Tejedor/The Eyes of the Weaver*
> *Pablo's Tree*

Grandmothers—Fiction
> *Abuela*
> *Las abuelas de Liliana*
> *Abuelita's Paradise*
> *Grandma Fina and Her Wonderful Umbrellas/La Abuelita Fina y sus sombrillas maravillosas*
> *Isla*
> *La isla*
> *Liliana's Grandmothers*
> *Magda's Tortillas/Las tortillas de Magda*
> *Mama Provi and the Pot of Rice*
> *El Paraíso de Abuelita*
> *The Tamale Quilt*
> *The Tortilla Quilt*

Grandparents—Fiction
> *Icy Watermelon/Sandía fría*

Great-aunts—Fiction
> *A Birthday Basket for Tía*
> *Una canasta de cumpleaños para Tía*

Hair—Fiction
> *Hairs/Pelitos*

Handicraft
> *Magic Windows/Ventanas mágicas*

Herrera, Juan Felipe/Childhood and Youth/Homes and Haunts—California
> *Calling the Doves/El canto de las palomas*
> *The Upside Down Boy/El niño de cabeza*

Hispanic American families—Texas—Kingsville
> *Family Pictures/Cuadros de familia*
> *In My Family/En mi familia*

Hispanic Americans—Fiction
> *Abuela*
> *Hairs/Pelitos*
> *Hooray! A Piñata!*
> *Isla*
> *La isla*
> *It Doesn't Have to Be This Way/No tiene que ser así*
> *Mama Provi and the Pot of Rice*
> *The Piñata Quilt*
> *Pepita Takes Time/Pepita, siempre tarde*
> *Pepita Talks Twice/Pepita habla dos veces*

Hispanic Americans—Fiction
> *Salsa*
> *The Tamale Quilt*
> *The Tortilla Quilt*
> *Viva! Una piñata!*

Hispanic Americans—Folklore
> *Fiesta U.S.A.*

Hispanic Americans—Social life and customs
> *Family Pictures/Cuadros de familia*
> *Fiesta U.S.A.*
> *In My Family/En mi familia*

Hispanic Americans—Texas—Kingsville—Social life and customs

> *Family Pictures/Cuadros de familia*
> *In My Family/En mi familia*

Holes—Fiction
> *Carlos Digs to China/Carlos excava hasta la China*

Pablo's Tree
*Pepita Thinks Pink/Pepita y el color
   rosado*
Qué montón de tamales!
¡Qué sorpresa de cumpleaños!
Radio Man/Don Radio
The Rainbow Tulip
Sip, Slurp, Soup, Soup/Caldo, caldo, caldo
Snapshots from the Wedding
Tomás and the Library Lady
Tomás y la señora de la biblioteca
Too Many Tamales

Mexican Americans—Poetry
*Angels Ride Bikes and Other Fall Poems/
   Los Ángeles Andan en Bicicleta y otros
   poemas de otoño*
An Elegy on the Death of César Chávez

Mexican Americans—San Francisco (Calif.)
Barrio

Mexican Americans—Social life and customs
Fiesta U.S.A.
Magic Windows/Ventanas mágicas

Mexico—Fiction
Chave's Memories/Los recuerdos de Chave

Mexico—Poetry
*From the Bellybutton of the Moon and
   Other Summer Poems/Del Ombligo de
   la Luna y otros poemas de verano*

Mexico—Social life and customs
Magic Windows/Ventanas mágicas

Mice—Fiction
Chato y su cena
Chato's Kitchen

Migrant agricultural laborers—Poetry
An Elegy on the Death of César Chávez

Migrant labor—California
Calling the Doves/El canto de las palomas

Migrant labor—Fiction
The Christmas Gift/El regalo de Navidad
Radio Man/Don Radio
Tomás and the Library Lady
Tomás y la señora de la biblioteca

Migrant labor—Poetry
An Elegy on the Death of César Chávez

Mission District (San Francisco, Calif.)—Social life and customs
Barrio

Money—Fiction
Carlos and the Carnival/Carlos y la feria

Mothers and daughters—Fiction
Big Enough/Bastante grande
Hairs/Pelitos

Mustaches—Fiction
Big Bushy Mustache

Nature—Poetry
*From the Bellybutton of the Moon and
   Other Summer Poems/Del Ombligo de
   la Luna y otros poemas de verano*
*Laughing Tomatoes and Other Spring
   Poems/Jitomates Risueños y otros poe-
   mas de primavera*

New Mexico—Fiction
*Carlos and the Cornfield/Carlos y la milpa
   de maíz*
Carlos and the Skunk/Carlos y el zorrillo
*Carlos and the Squash Plant/Carlos y la
   planta de calabaza*
Farolitos for Abuelo
The Farolitos of Christmas
*Los Ojos del Tejedor/The Eyes of the
   Weaver*

New York (N.Y.)—Fiction
Abuela

Paper work
Magic Windows/Ventanas mágicas

Spanish language materials

Abuela
Las abuelas de Liliana
Barrio: El barrio de José
Una canasta de cumpleaños para Tía
Chato y su cena
Fiesta U.S.A.
Gorrión del metro
La Isla
La llaman América
La Mariposa
Un mundo nuevo
El Paraíso de Abuelita
Qué montón de tamales!
¡Qué sorpresa de cumpleaños!
Tomás y la señora de la biblioteca
Viva! Una piñata!

Spanish language materials—Bilingual

The Adventures of Connie and Diego/Los aventuras de Connie y Diego
Angels Ride Bikes and Other Fall Poems/ Los Ángeles Andan en Bicicleta y otros poemas de otoño
Benito's Bizcochitos/Los bizcochitos de Benito
Big Enough/Bastante grande
Calling the Doves/El canto de las palomas
Carlos and the Carnival/Carlos y la feria
Carlos and the Cornfield/Carlos y la milpa de maíz
Carlos and the Skunk/Carlos y el zorrillo
Carlos and the Squash Plant/Carlos y la planta de calabaza
Carlos Digs to China/Carlos excava hasta la China
Chave's Memories/Los recuerdos de Chave
The Christmas Gift/El regalo de Navidad
The Christmas Tree/El árbol de Navidad
Family, Familia
Family Pictures/Cuadros de familia
Friends from the Other Side/Amigos del otro lado
From the Bellybutton of the Moon and Other Summer Poems/Del Ombligo de la Luna y otros poemas de verano

A Gift from Papá Diego/Un regalo de Papá Diego
Grandma Fina and Her Wonderful Umbrellas/La Abuelita Fina y sus sombrillas maravillosas
Hairs/Pelitos
Icy Watermelon/Sandía fría
In My Family/En mi familia
It Doesn't Have to Be This Way/No tiene que ser así
Laughing Tomatoes and Other Spring Poems/Jitomates Risueños y otros poemas de primavera
Magda's Tortillas/Las tortillas de Magda
Magic Windows/Ventanas mágicas
My Aunt Otilia's Spirits/Los espíritus de mi Tía Otilia
My Very Own Room/Mi propio cuartito
Pepita Takes Time/Pepita, siempre tarde
Pepita Talks Twice/Pepita habla dos veces
Pepita Thinks Pink/Pepita y el color rosado
Radio Man/Don Radio
Salsa
Sip, Slurp, Soup, Soup/Caldo, caldo, caldo
The Upside Down Boy/El niño de cabeza

Spanish language—Readers

The Adventures of Connie and Diego/Los aventuras de Connie y Diego
My Aunt Otilia's Spirits/Los espíritus de mi Tía Otilia

Spring—Poetry

Laughing Tomatoes and Other Spring Poems/Jitomates Risueños y otros poemas de primavera

Squashes—Fiction

Carlos and the Squash Plant/Carlos y la planta de calabaza

Stealing—Fiction

Big Enough/Bastante grande

Stories in rhyme

The Christmas Tree/El árbol de Navidad

Storytelling—Fiction

Chave's Memories/Los recuerdos de Chave

Subways—Fiction

Gorrión del metro
Subway Sparrow

Summer—Poetry

*From the Bellybutton of the Moon and
    Other Summer Poems/Del Ombligo de
    la Luna y otros poemas de verano*

Tardiness—Fiction

Pepita Takes Time/Pepita, siempre tarde

Texas—Fiction

*Friends from the Other Side/Amigos del
    otro lado*

Tortillas—Fiction

Magda's Tortillas/Las tortillas de Magda
Sip, Slurp, Soup, Soup/Caldo, caldo, caldo

Twins—Fiction

*The Adventures of Connie and Diego/Los
    aventuras de Connie y Diego*

Umbrellas and parasols—Fiction

*Grandma Fina and Her Wonderful
    Umbrellas/La Abuelita Fina y sus som-
    brillas maravillosas*

**United States—Religious life and
customs**

Fiesta U.S.A.

United States—Social life and customs

Fiesta U.S.A.

Watermelon—Fiction

Icy Watermelon/Sandía fría

Weaving—Fiction

Los Ojos del Tejedor/The Eyes of the Weaver

Weddings—Fiction

Snapshots from the Wedding

Part V

Literary and Artistic Awards/Lists of Recommended Books

Many of the picture books listed in Part II have been recognized with awards and prizes. Others titles have been nominated for prestigious awards, and while they did not win the top honor, they nonetheless deserve of recognition. The fact that a title has been included in a list of recommended books is also an honor.

It is impossible to include all such honors from across the United States, but the major awards have been included. The reader should remember that the process is ongoing, with new awards being conferred frequently. Obviously, recently published titles have not yet had the opportunity to receive awards, which may be forthcoming. This section lists awards with brief explanations. These listings should not be considered an endorsement of any particular review source or organization.

ALA Notable Children's Books
<http://www.ala.org/alsc/notablebooks_terms.html>
Titles on this annual list from the American Library Association should be "worthy of note or notice, important, distinguished, outstanding." These books should have literary quality, be original in text and illustrations, and have clarity and style of language. The illustrations, design, and format should be excellent. Titles should be of interest, have value, and be acceptable to children.

2001	*Chato and the Party Animals*
2001	*The Christmas Gift/El regalo de Navidad*
1997	*Family Pictures/Cuadros de familia*
1996	*Chato's Kitchen*
pre-1996	*Abuela*

Américas Award
<http://www.uwm.edu/Dept/CLACS/outreach_americas.html>
The Américas awards recognize U.S. works of fiction, poetry, folklore or nonfiction, published in English or Spanish, that authentically and engagingly portray Latin America, the Caribbean, or Latinos in the United States. The Consortium of Latin American Studies Programs (CLASP) at the University of Wisconsin-Milwaukee sponsors this award.

2000 honorable mention	*My Very Own Room/Mi propio cuartito*
2000 commended	*The Christmas Gift/El regalo de Navidad*
2000 commended	*Icy Watermelon/Sandía fría*
1999 honorable mention	*Magic Windows/Ventanas mágicas*
1999 commended	*Angels Ride Bikes and Other Fall Poems/Los Ángeles Andan en Bicicleta y otros poemas de otoño*
1999 commended	*It Doesn't Have to Be This Way/No tiene que ser así*
1998 winner	*Barrio*
1998 commended	*Big Bushy Mustache*
1998 commended	*From the Bellybutton of the Moon and Other Summer Poems/Del Ombligo de la Luna y otros poemas de verano*
1998 commended	*Liliana's Grandmothers*
1998 commended	*La Mariposa*
1997 commended	*The Birthday Swap*
1997 commended	*Carlos and the Skunk/Carlos y el zorrillo*
1997 commended	*Laughing Tomatoes and Other Spring Poems/Jitomates Risueños y otros poemas de primavera*
1997 commended	*Tomás and the Library Lady*
1996 winner	*In My Family/En mi familia*
1996 commended	*Chave's Memories/Las recuerdos de Chave*
1996 commended	*Hooray, a Piñata!*
1995 honorable mention	*Chato's Kitchen*
1995 commended	*Calling the Doves/El canto de las palomas*
1995 commended	*The Farolitos of Christmas*
1995 commended	*Fiesta U.S.A.*
1995 commended	*Isla*
1994 honorable mention	*Pablo's Tree*
1993 honorable mention	*Radio Man/Don Radio*

Booklist Editors' Choice Books for Youth
<http://www.ala.org/booklist/>
Booklist is a magazine published by the American Library Association. *Booklist* includes book reviews and reviews of electronic media.

1997	*Snapshots from the Wedding*
1996	*Hooray, a Piñata!*

Bulletin of the Center for Children's Books, Blue Ribbon Books
<http://www.lis.uiuc.edu/puboff/bccb>

The Center for Children's Books is affiliated with the Graduate School of Library and Information Science at the University of Illinois. *The Bulletin* is a children's book review journal for school and public librarians. Since 1990 Blue Ribbon books have been chosen annually by the staff of the Center in Champaign, Illinois.

1997 *Snapshots from the Wedding*

California Department of Education, Recommended Literature List
<http://www.cde.ca.gov/cdepress/pubs/english_lang_arts2.html>

The lists of recommendations are found in several books from CDE Press, a division of the California Department of Education. These lists are available for purchase.

Abuela
Calling the Doves/El canto de las palomas
The Rainbow Tulip
Tomás and the Library Lady
Too Many Tamales

California Young Reader Medal Reading List
<http://cateweb.org/cyrm.html>

In a program sponsored by the California Association of Teachers of English, the California Library Association, the California Reading Association, and the California School Library Association, the students of California nominate and select the winners of this medal.

2000 nominee *Mama Provi and the Pot of Rice*
1997 nominee *Chato's Kitchen*

Ezra Jack Keats Award
<http://www.nypl.org/admin/pro/press/keats99.html>

The Ezra Jack Keats Award is the responsibility of the Ezra Jack Keats Foundation. The award is named in honor of Ezra Jack Keats, a book author and artist who won the Caldecott Medal for his book *The Snowy Day*. The award is given each year to an outstanding new writer of picture books for children age nine and under. The award is presented by the Foundation and the New York Public Library.

1997 *Calling the Doves/El canto de las palomas*

Georgia Book Award
<http://www.coe.uga.edu/gachildlit/awards/index.html>

The Georgia Book Award program began in 1968 with the language education faculty of the University of Georgia's College of Education. The goal of the program is to acquaint children with the joys of reading for pleasure. Georgia teachers and librarians nominate fiction book titles, and students in pre-kindergarten through fourth grade select winners.

2000–2001 nominee	*Mama Provi and the Pot of Rice*
2000–2001 nominee	*Tomás and the Library Lady*
1999–2000 nominee	*Liliana's Grandmothers*

International Reading Association Notable Books
<http://www.reading.org/choices/>
The purpose of the International Reading Association is to promote high levels of literacy for all. It serves as a clearinghouse for reading research and encourages lifetime reading. *Choices* is an annual publication that includes annotated entries for children's and young adult books.

Children's Choices is co-sponsored by the Children's Book Council and the International Reading Association. The list appears in the October issue of *The Reading Teacher*.

> *From the Bellybutton of the Moon and Other Summer Poems/*
>   *Del Ombligo de la Luna y otros poemas de verano*
> *The Birthday Swap*
> *Calling the Doves/El canto de las palomas*
> *When This World Was New*

Teachers' Choices is selected by teachers, librarians, and reading specialists. The list of 30 titles is published in the November issue of *The Reading Teacher*.

> *Calling the Doves/El canto de las palomas*
> *In My Family/En mi familia*

Missouri Show Me Readers Award, Reader/Selectors List
The purpose of the Show Me Readers Award is to promote reading, literacy, and literature in Missouri. This award is a children's choice award sponsored by the Missouri Association of School Librarians. Students in grades one, two, and three read at least six books from a master list and vote in March for the book they liked best.

1999–2000 for 2000–2001 school year	*Big Bushy Mustache*

National Council for the Social Studies (NCSS)

Carter G. Woodson Award
<http://www.ncss.org/awards/woodsonlist.html>
This award honors the memory of Carter G. Woodson, an African-American historian, educator, and writer. This award, established in 1974 by NCSS, intends to encourage the writing, publishing, and dissemination of outstanding social science books that treat topics related to minorities sensitively and accurately.

2000	*Magic Windows/Ventanas mágicas*

Notable Social Studies Books
<http://www.ncss.org/resources/notable/home.html>
Books on this list were evaluated and selected by a committee of NCSS in cooperation with The Children's Book Council. This bibliography has been published annually since 1972.

2001	*The Christmas Gift/El regalo de Navidad*
2000	*Farolitos for Abuelo*
1999	*Barrio*
pre-1998	*Abuela*

National Parenting Publications, Gold Medal or Honors Award
<http://www.parenthoodweb.com/articles/phw1190.htm>
The National Parenting Publications Awards (NAPPA) program started in 1990. It is a consumer awards program for children's media. Awards include toys, music, videocassettes, and software as well as books. Judges review and select winners, which are announced annually.

> *Laughing Tomatoes and Other Spring Poems/Jitomates Risueños y otros poemas de primavera*
> *Hairs/Pelitos*

Nebraska Golden Sower Award
<http://www.nol.org/home/NLA/golden/sower.htm>
The Nebraska Library Association sponsors this program. Awards are given in three categories: picture book (kindergarten through grade 3), grades 4 through 6, and young adult. This award was first presented in 1981, with the picture book portion beginning in 1983. The award is presented annually. Purposes of these awards are to stimulate thinking, introduce types of literature, encourage independent reading, increase library skills, and foster an appreciation of excellent writing and illustrating.

> Nominee   *Tomás and the Library Lady*

New Mexico Land of Enchantment Award
<http://www.stlibstate.nm.us/youth/LandInfo.html>
The purpose of this award is to encourage children of New Mexico to read more and better books. It was first presented in 1981. It is sponsored by the New Mexico Library Association and the New Mexico Reading Association. The winner is chosen by children in New Mexico in grades four through eight. A master list is assembled annually by a selection committee.

> **1998–1999** nominee   *Carlos and the Cornfield/Carlos y la milpa de maíz*

New York Public Library "100 Picture Books Everyone Should Know"

<http://www.nypl.org/branch/kids/gloria.html>

This list is formulated by librarians at the New York Public Library.

> *Abuela*

North Carolina Children's Book Award

<http://www.lib.co.rowan.nc.us/KidsStuff/BookAward/NCBookAward.htm>

The North Carolina Association of School Librarians and the Children's Services Section of the North Carolina Library Association sponsor this program to encourage students to become acquainted with the best writers, to broaden awareness of literature, to promote reading aloud, and to recognize and honor favorite books and authors.

> **2000–2001** nominee   *Mama Provi and the Pot of Rice*

Notable Books for a Global Society

<http://www.csulb.edu/org/childrens-lit/Projects/
Notable_Books_for_a_Global_Soc/notable_books%2Aa_global_soc.html>

Developed by the Notable Books for a Global Society Committee of the Children's Literature and Reading Special Interest Group of the International Reading Association, this list of books was selected as outstanding K–12 multicultural literature.

> **1997**   *In My Family/En mi familia*

Parents' Choice

<http://www.parents-choice.org>

The Parents' Choice Foundation was formed at Radcliffe College in 1975 and became a legal entity in 1978. The purpose is to help mothers and fathers guide their children by providing reviews of children's media.

> **2001**   *Icy Watermelon/Sandía fría*
> **2000**   *Family Pictures/Cuadros de familia*
> **2000**   *Hairs/Pelitos*
> **1999**   *Angels Ride Bikes and Other Fall Poems/*
> *Los Ángeles Andan en Bicicleta y otros poemas de otoño*
> **1999**   *It Doesn't Have to Be This Way/No tiene que ser así*
> **1999**   *Magic Windows/Ventanas mágicas*
> **1999**   *La Mariposa*
> **pre-1999**   *Abuela*
> **pre-1999**   *Chato's Kitchen*

Paterson Prize for Books for Young People

<http://www.pccc.cc.nj.us/poetry/winers2000.htm>

The Paterson Prize for Books for Young People is awarded annually by the Poetry Center at Passaic County Community College in Paterson, New Jersey.

1999   *América Is Her Name*

Pura Belpré Award

<http://www.ala.org/alsc/belpre.html>

The Pura Belpré Award was established in 1996 to recognize Latino/Latina writers and illustrators whose works portray, affirm, and celebrate the Latino cultural experience in outstanding works of literature for children and youth. It is co-sponsored by the Association for Library Service to Children (ALSC), a division of the American Library Association (ALA), and the National Association to Promote Library Services to the Spanish Speaking (REFORMA). Named for Pura Belpré, the first Latina librarian at the New York Public Library, awards are given biennially.

2000 winner for illustration	*Magic Windows/Ventanas mágicas*
2000 honor book for narrative	*From the Bellybutton of the Moon and Other Summer Poems/Del Ombligo de la Luna y otros poemas de verano*
2000 winner for illustration	*Barrio*
1998 winner for illustration	*Snapshots from the Wedding*
1998 honor book for narrative	*Laughing Tomatoes and Other Spring Poems/ Jitomates Risueños y otros poemas de primavera*
1998 honor book for illustration	*In My Family/En mi familia*
1996 winner for illustration	*Chato's Kitchen*
1996 honor book for illustration	*Family Pictures/Cuadros de familia*

Scholastic's 200 for 2000: Literature for the Millennium

<http://www.freep.com/fun/books/books13_19991213.htm>

This list, created in 1999 in anticipation of the turn of the century, was compiled by editors at Scholastic Publishing.

Chato's Kitchen
Tomás and the Library Lady
Family Pictures/Cuadros de familia

Schon, Dr. Isabel

<http://www.csusm.edu/csb>

Dr. Isabel Schon, director of the Barahona Center for the Study of Books in Spanish for Children and Adolescents at California State University, San Marcos, is the author of several books from Scarecrow Press. The following boldfaced titles contain information on the picture books in this guide.

Recommended Books in Spanish for Children and Young Adults, 1991–1995:
Carlos and the Cornfield/Carlos y la milpa de maíz
Gorrión del metro

Recommended Books in Spanish for Children and Young Adults, 1996–1999:
¡Qué sorpresa de cumpleaños!
Chato y su cena
From the Bellybutton of the Moon and Other Summer Poems/
Del Ombligo de la Luna y otros poemas de verano
Viva! Una piñata!
In My Family/En mi familia
Laughing Tomatoes and Other Spring Poems/Jitomates Risueños y otros poemas de primavera
Las abuelas de Liliana
Tomás y la señora de la biblioteca
Qué montón de tamales!

The Best of the Latino Heritage:
Abuela
Barrio: El barrio de José
Family Pictures/Cuadros de familia
The Farolitos of Christmas

Skipping Stones
<http://www.treelink.com/skipping/index.html>
Skipping Stones is a nonprofit, multicultural children's magazine published bimonthly during the school year. The magazine contains pen pal information, book reviews, news, and a guide for parents and teachers. Award winning books are selected by a committee of reviewers including editors, librarians, parents, students, and teachers.

2001 honor	*Elegy on the Death of César Chávez*
2001 honor	*My Very Own Room/Mi propio cuartito*
2000 honor	*It Doesn't Have to Be This Way/No tiene que ser así*
2000 honor	*Magic Windows/Ventanas mágicas*
1999 honor	*América Is Her Name*
1999 honor	*From the Bellybutton of the Moon and Other Summer Poems/Del Ombligo de la Luna y otros poemas de verano*
1998 honor	*Tomás and the Library Lady*
1997 honor	*In My Family/En mi familia*
1996 honor	*Pepita Talks Twice/Pepita habla dos veces*

Smithsonian Notable Books for Children
<http://www.smithsonianmag.si.edu/>
Smithsonian Magazine is a monthly publication of the Smithsonian, a collection of museums, galleries, a zoo, and research facilities with the purpose of preserving the achievements of humankind. Notable Books Lists are published in November.

2000	*The Upside Down Boy/El niño de cabeza*
1999	*It Doesn't Have to Be This Way/No tiene que ser así*
1998	*La Mariposa*
1997	*Tomás and the Library Lady*
1995	*Calling the Doves/El canto de las palomas*

Texas Bluebonnet Award
<http://www.txla.org/groups/tba/index.html>

The Texas Bluebonnet Award is co-sponsored by the Children's Round Table of the Texas Library Association and the Texas Association of School Librarians. It was first awarded in 1981. A master list of 15 to 20 titles is prepared by the administrative committee from nominations by librarians, teachers, parents, and students. Texas students in grades three through six who have read or heard at least five of the titles are eligible to vote for their favorite. The title that receives the highest number of votes is the winner.

2001–2002	*The Upside Down Boy/El niño de cabeza*
1999–2000	*Tomás and the Library Lady*
1998–1999	*Family Pictures/Cuadros de familia*
1997–1998	*In My Family/En mi familia*

Tomás Rivera Mexican American Children's Book Award
<http://www.education.swt.edu/Rivera/mainpage.html>

Tomás Rivera, a native of Crystal City, Texas, was born into a family of migrant farm workers and became a pioneer in Mexican-American literature with his *. . . y no se lo trago la tierra/. . . And the Earth Did Not Part*. He was an educator, university administrator, and tireless promoter of Mexican-American literature until his untimely death in 1984. The Tomás Rivera Children's Book Award was established in 1995 by Southwest Texas State University to encourage production of Mexican-American literature. It is awarded annually to authors and illustrators whose books for children and young adults authentically reflect the lives and experiences of Mexican Americans in the Southwest United States. Awards are made annually during Hispanic Heritage Month.

2000 nominee	*Elegy on the Death of César Chávez*
2000 nominee	*Magda's Tortillas/Las tortillas de Magda*
2000 nominee	*Icy Watermelon/Sandía fría*
2000 nominee	*The Upside Down Boy/El niño de cabeza*
2000 nominee	*The Christmas Gift/El regalo de Navidad*
2000 nominee	*Pepita Takes Time/Pepita, siempre tarde*
2000 nominee	*My Very Own Room/Mi propio cuartito*
2000 nominee	*Chato and the Party Animals*
1999 nominee	*Angels Ride Bikes and Other Fall Poems/ Los Ángeles Andan en Bicicleta y otros poemas de otoño*
1999 nominee	*Farolitos for Abuelo*
1999 nominee	*Benito's Bizcochitos/Los bizcochitos de Benito*

1999 nominee	*Grandma Fina and Her Wonderful Umbrellas/*
	La Abuelita Fina y sus sombrillas maravillosas
1999 nominee	*Family, Familia*
1999 nominee	*Magic Windows/Ventanas mágicas*
1999 nominee	*The Rainbow Tulip*
1999 nominee	*It Doesn't Have to Be This Way/No tiene que ser así*
1999 nominee	*The Piñata Quilt*
1998 nominee	*From the Bellybutton of the Moon and Other Summer*
	Poems/Del Ombligo de la Luna y otros poemas de verano
1998 nominee	*La Mariposa*
1998 nominee	*Big Enough/Bastante grande*
1998 nominee	*Pepita Thinks Pink/Pepita y el color rosado*
1998 nominee	*A Gift From Papá Diego/Un regalo de Papá Diego*
1997 winner	*Tomás and the Library Lady*
1997 nominee	*Laughing Tomatoes and Other Spring Poems/*
	Jitomates Risueños y otros poemas de primavera
1997 nominee	*Sip, Slurp, Soup, Soup/Caldo, caldo, caldo*
1997 nominee	*Tomás and the Library Lady*
1997 nominee	*Snapshots from the Wedding*
1996 winner	*In My Family/En mi familia*
1996 nominee	*Chave's Memories/Los recuerdos de Chave*
1996 nominee	*The Tortilla Quilt*
1995 winner	*Chato's Kitchen*
1995 nominee	*The Farolitos of Christmas*
1995 nominee	*Calor*
1995 nominee	*Pepita Talks Twice/Pepita habla dos veces*

Part VI

Publishing Companies, Distributors, and Related Organizations

The picture books included in Part II should be available from many sources including bookstores, both actual and virtual, and book jobbers. Some titles are provided directly from the publisher while others are not. This section lists some publishers and distributors for readers wishing to learn more about these and other books.

Publishers often provide catalogs, supplemental materials, and virtual information about authors, illustrators, and titles that may be of interest. Addresses, telephone numbers, e-mail addresses, and so forth are included for the reader's convenience, but are subject to change. For the larger publishers, names of contact persons for those wishing to arrange author visits have been provided, but are also subject to change.

Aladdin   *See* Simon & Schuster

Albert Whitman & Company
> 6340 Oakton Street, Morton Grove, IL 60053
> **Telephone:** 847-581-0033, 800-255-7675   **Fax:** 847-581-0039
> **E-mail:** mail@awhitmanco.com   **Web site:** <http://www.awhitmanco.com/>
>> Founded in 1919, Albert Whitman & Company is an independent publisher of children's books. Current topics include books on divorce, disabilities, and interracial families. Their online catalog lists concept books, multicultural books, holiday books, and others.

Atheneum   *See* Simon & Schuster

Bilingual Books for Kids Inc.
> P.O. Box 653, Ardsley, New York 10501-0653
> **Fax:** 1-800-385-1020
> **E-mail:** bilingualbooks@mindspring.com   **Web site:** <http://www.bilingualbooks.com/>

Bilingual Books for Kids distributes bilingual books for children. Their inventory includes original bilingual books and translations of English-language titles.

Bookstore of the Americas

3020 27th Ave. South, Minneapolis, MN 55406
Telephone: 612-276-0801, 800-452-8382
E-mail: Bookstore@americas.org   **Web site:** <http://www.americas.org/Store>
The Bookstore of the Americas is a program of the Resource Center of the Americas, a non-profit human rights organization that provides educational materials about border issues. It offers books in English, Spanish, and bilingual editions and curriculum materials.

Children's Book Press

2211 Mission Street, San Francisco, CA 94110
Telephone: 415-821-3080   **Fax:** 415- 821-3081
E-mail: info@cbookpress@cbookpress.org   **Web site:** http://www.cbookpress.org.
Children's Book Press is a nonprofit publisher founded in 1975 by Harriet Rohmer. Publishing multicultural literature for children, the Press seeks to encourage an international multicultural perspective in young readers. Information about books and about LitLinks, an educational outreach program involving authors and illustrators, is provided on the Web site.

Cinco Puntos Press

2709 Louisville, El Paso, TX 79930
Telephone: 915-566-9072   **Fax:** 915-565-5335
E-mail: leebyrd@cincopuntos.com   **Web site:** <http://www.cincopuntos.com>
Cinco Puntos Press has received an American Book Award from the Before Columbus Foundation, the Latino Literary Hall of Fame, a Sunshine Community Service Award for a lifetime commitment to literature, the Dwight A. Myers Award for excellence in regional publishing, and a Southwest Book Award for excellence in publishing.

Clear Light Publications

823 Don Diego, Santa Fe, NM 87501
Telephone: 1-888-253-2747   **Fax:** 1-505-989-9519
E-mail: service@clearlightbooks.com   **Web site:** <http://www.clearlightbooks.com>
Clear Light is a regional publisher with catalogs of Hispanic and Native American titles as well as art, religion, philosophy, cookbooks, western Americana, and more.

Curbstone Press

321 Jackson Street, Willimantic, CT 06226
Telephone: 860-423-5110   **Fax:** 860-423-9242
E-mail: info@curbstone.org   **Web site:** <http://www.curbstone.org>
Curbstone Press is a nonprofit publisher dedicated to literature that reflects a commitment to social change with emphasis on writing from Latin America and Latinos in the United States. Curbstone publishes eight to ten titles per year.

Dragonfly Books   *See* Random House

Dutton Children's Books   *See* Penguin Putnam

Econo-Clad Books

Telephone: 800-255-3502   **Fax:** 800-628-2410

E-mail: info@sagebrushcorp.com   **Web site:** <http://www.sagebrushcorp.com/books/>

Econo-Clad is a division of Sagebrush Corporation, a library and information services company. Econo-Clad produces pre-bound versions of many of the titles in this guide. Their Web site includes areas for librarians and teachers, complimentary posters, and a searchable online catalog. Paper catalogs with specific titles, such as Accelerated Reader and Reading Counts, are available.

Farrar, Straus, Giroux

19 Union Square West, New York, NY 10003

Fax: 212-633-2427

E-mail: Childrens-marketing@fsgee.com   **Web site:** <http://fsbassociates.com/fsg/>

Contact person for author visits: Jeanne T. McDermott, Assistant Director of Marketing, Telephone: 212-741-6900

Farrar, Straus, Giroux was founded in New York in 1945. They publish children's and adult titles including poetry and novels.

Harcourt Children's Books

525 B Street, Suite 1900, San Diego, CA 92101

Fax: 619-699-6777 or 800-221-2477

E-mail: booksforkids@harcourt.com   **Web site:** <http://www.harcourt.com/>

Contact person for author visits: Kia Neri, Author Promotions Coordinator, Telephone: 616-699-5234

Harcourt Children's Books provides teaching resources, lesson plans, and articles about children's books and literature for kids, parents, teens, and educators.

Harper (HarperCollins)

1350 Avenue of the Americas, New York, NY 10019

Telephone: 212-261-6500

Web site: <http://www.harperchildrens.com>

Contact person for author visits: Catherine Balkin, Library Promotions Manager, Telephone: 212-207-7450

HarperCollins' imprints include Avon, Joanna Cotler, Laura Geringer, Greenwillow, HarperTrophy, HarperTempest, and HarperFestival books. An online newsletter for parents and educators, and reading group guides are available. Kids may want to check out the "Have Some Fun" activities on the Web site.

Hispanic Book Distributors

240 E. Yvon Drive, Tucson, AZ 85704

Telephone: 520-293-2976   **Fax:** 520-407-0744

E-mail: hbdus@cs.com   **Web site:** <http://www.hispanicbooks.com>

Hispanic Book Distributors provides Spanish-language books, cassettes, and children's books in bilingual, Spanish, and English-language formats.

The Trejo Foster Foundation for Hispanic Library Education is allied with Hispanic Book Distributors. Information about the foundation and its Reformita club is available to teachers and librarians by calling or writing.

Houghton Mifflin

215 Park Ave. South, New York, NY 10003
Fax: 212-420-5850 or 617-351-1109
Web sites: Education Place <http://www.eduplace.com/aboutus.html>
Kids Place <http://www.eduplace.com/kids/index.html>
Parents' Place <http://www.eduplace.com/parents/index.html>
Contact person for author visits: Justin Barclay, Marketing Associate, Telephone: 617-351-5903
Houghton Mifflin's Web sites offer activities, resources, educational games, and discussion
forums. Numerous, specific e-mail addresses are listed on the site.

Hyperion Books Disney Publishing Worldwide

114 Fifth Avenue, New York, NY 10011
Telephone: 212-633-4400
Web site: <http://www.hyperionbooks.com/> or
<http://disney.go.com/disneybooks/hyperionbooks/homepage.html>
Contact person for author visits: Lauren L. Wohl, Marketing Director, Telephone 212-633-4433
Hyperion, founded in 1991, is a part of Disney Publishing Worldwide.

Knopf   *See* Random House

Lectorum Publications

137 West 14th Street, New York, NY
Telephone: 212-741-0220   **Fax:** 877-532-8676
E-mail: lectorum@scholastic.com   **Web site:** <http://www.lectorum.com/>
Lectorum, a Spanish-language division of Scholastic, is a distributor, publisher of translations, and bookstore. Lectorum sells to schools, libraries, and bookstores. An online order
form may be faxed. An online inquiry form is available for readers wishing to request catalogs, ask questions, and make comments.

Lee & Low Books

95 Madison Avenue, New York, NY 10016
Telephone: 888-320-3395   **Fax:** 212-683-1894
E-mail: info@leeandlow.com   **Web site:** <http://www.leeandlow.com/home/index.html>
Lee & Low Books publishes multicultural literature for children. Their friendly Web site
includes active learner classroom guides, booktalks, a calendar, and more.

Libros Sin Fronteras

P.O. Box 2085, Olympia, WA 98507
Telephone: 360-357-4332   **Fax:** 360-357-4964
E-mail: info@librossinfronteras.com   **Web site:** <http://www.librossinfronteras.com/index.html>
Libros Sin Fronteras is a bilingual company that distributes Latin American and Spanish-
language materials. Their products include books, books on tape, and music.

Lodestar Books   *See* Penguin

Macmillan   *See* Simon & Schuster

Northland   *See* Rising Moon

PaperStar   *See* Penguin Putnam

Penguin Putnam
375 Hudson Street, New York, NY 10014
Mail orders: 405 Murray Hill Parkway, East Rutherford, NJ 07073
Telephone: 800-788-6262 (orders)
Web site: <http://www.penguinputnam.com>
Contact person for author visits for Dutton, G.P. Putnam's, Lodestar, and Viking: Skye
Stewart, Author Appearance Coordinator, Telephone: 212-366-2457
The Penguin Group, the second-largest English-language trade book publisher in the world,
includes children's imprints: Dial Books, Dutton, Grosset & Dunlap, Philomel, Puffin, G. P.
Putnam's Sons, Viking, and Frederick Warne. The Web site features a searchable online cata-
log and offers young readers reading guides, author and illustrator information, and free
stuff. Fax numbers for individual imprints are listed on the site.

Piñata Books (Arte Público)
U. of Houston 4800 Calhoun, Houston, TX 77204-2174
Telephone: 713-743-2998, 800-633-ARTE
Web site: <http://www.arte.uh.edu>
Arte Público, publisher of contemporary and recovered literature by U.S. Hispanic authors,
was founded in 1979 by Nicolás Kanellos. The press publishes 30 titles per year by Latino
authors. Piñata Books, the children's and young adult imprint of Arte Público, began publi-
cation in 1994.

Quarter Inch Designs & Publishing (1/4 Inch)
33255 Stoneman Street #B, Lake Elsinore, CA 92530
Telephone: 909-609-3309   **Fax:** 909-609-3369
Web site: <http://www.QuarterInchPublishing.com>
Freelance artist Jane Tenorio-Coscarelli owns Quarter Inch Designs & Publishing. Books are
available for purchase directly from the publisher and through distributors. A form for sub-
mitting comments is available on her Web site.

Random House
280 Park Avenue (11-3), New York, NY 10017
Fax: 212-940-7381
Web site: <http://www.randomhouse.com>
Contact person for author visits for Knopf and Random: Kerry Ryan MacManus, Public
Relations Manager, Telephone: 212-940-7608
The largest English-language general trade book publisher in the world, Random House
includes children's imprints Alfred A. Knopf, Bantam, Crown, Delacorte, Disney,
Doubleday, Dragonfly, Laurel-Leaf, Lucas, Random House, Sesame Workshop, Wendy
Lamb, and Yearling. The Web site includes areas for kids, teens, parents, teachers, and
librarians. They offer downloadable seasonal catalogs, a mailing list sign-up, guides, and
author information.

Renaissance Learning (formerly Advantage Learning)

P.O. Box 8036, Wisconsin Rapids, WI 54495-8036

Telephone: 888-656-2931, 715-424-3636 **Fax:** 715-424-4242

E-mail: answers@renlearn.com **Web site:** <http://www.renlearn.com>

Renaissance Learning offers professional development seminars, and math, writing, and reading software, including the Accelerated Reader materials.

Rising Moon (Northland Publishing)

P.O. Box 1389, Flagstaff, AZ 86002-1389

Telephone: 800-346-3257 **Fax:** 1-800-257-9082

E-mail: info@northlandpub.com **Web site:** <http://www.northlandpub.com>

Rising Moon is the children's division of Northland Publishing. The Web site offers Tools for Teachers & Librarians, educational and copyright-free supplements with learning and extension activities that might also interest parents. School and library discounts are available.

Scholastic Reading Counts

555 Broadway, New York, NY 10012-3999

Web site: <http://src.scholastic.com/ecatalog/readingcounts/index.htm>

Scholastic publishes books, provides book fairs, and is the supplier of Reading Counts computerized tests. They also sell many of the Reading Counts books from other publishers. Their Web site contains areas for parents, teachers, and kids.

Simon & Schuster

1230 Avenue of the Americas, New York, NY 10020

Web site: <http://www.simonandschuster.com>

Contact person for author visits at Atheneum: Jennifer Stephenson, Author Appearance Coordinator, Telephone: 212-698-2803

Contact person for author visits at Simon & Schuster: Lisa McClatchy, Author Appearance Coordinator, Telephone: 212-698-2300; E-mail: authorappearances@simonandschuster.com

Imprints in the children's division include Books for Young Readers, Aladdin, Little Simon, Simon Spotlight, Margaret K. McElderry, and Atheneum. The Web site includes title and author information, a librarian update, teacher's guides, reading group guides, activity kits, online forms, and more.

Small Press Distribution

1342 Seventh Street, Berkeley, CA 94710-1409

Telephone: 510-524-1668, 800-869-7553 **Fax:** 510-869-7553

Web site: <http://www.spdbooks.org/>

Small Press Distribution is the only nonprofit book wholesaler in the United States. Founded in 1969, it provides wholesaling services for 432 presses, offers public programs and advocacy, and is devoted exclusively to independently published literature, including poetry and fiction by African Americans, Asian Americans, Native Americans, Latinas/Latinos, and gay/lesbian writers.

Viking *See* Penguin Putnam

Part VII

A Bibliography of Additional Latino-Related Books

During the compilation of the titles in Part II, some titles did not fit for various reasons. Some had settings in countries other than the United States. Others featured Latino characters but were written by non-Latino writers. Despite the fact that these titles did not meet all the criteria to be included in Part II, they may be of interest, depending on the individual reader's requirements. Some titles in this bibliography may be out of print or otherwise unavailable for purchase. Readers who are interested in additional picture books are encouraged to consider the titles in this bibliography and do research to determine which books will best meet their needs.

Abuelito Eats with His Fingers by Janice Levy, illustrated by Layne Johnson. Eakin Press, 1999.
Cristina is uncomfortable around her Spanish-speaking grandfather until she spends the day with him and he helps her to begin to understand his culture and her family.

Alejandro's Gift by Richard E. Albert, illustrated by Sylvia Long. Chronicle Books, 1994.
Lonely in his house in the desert, Alejandro builds an oasis to attract animals.

Amelia's Road by Linda Jacobs Altman, illustrated by Enrique O. Sánchez. Lee & Low Books, 1993.
Tired of moving, Amelia, daughter of migrant farm workers, dreams of a stable home.

Amigo by Byrd Baylor, illustrated by Garth Williams. Aladdin Books, 1963, 1989.
Wanting a pet, a boy decides to tame a prairie dog who has decided to tame the boy.

Angel's Kite/La estella de Ángel by Alberto Blanco, pictures by Rodolfo Morales, English translation by Dan Bellm. Children's Book Press/Libros para niños, 1994.
A boy makes a kite that mysteriously restores a long-missing bell to the town church.

Anthony Reynoso: Born to Rope by Martha Cooper and Ginger Gordon. Clarion, 1996.
The experiences of Tony as he follows in the Mexican trick roping tradition are documented.

Bajo la luna de limón by Edith Hope Fine, illustrated by René King Moreno, translated by Eida de la Vega. Lee & Low Books, 1999.
This is the Spanish version of *Under the Lemon Moon*.

Born in the Gravy by Denys Cazet. Orchard Books, 1993, 1997.
A Mexican-American girl tells her father about her first day of kindergarten.

Butterfly Boy by Virginia Kroll, illustrated by Gerardo Suzán. Boyds Mills, 1997.
A boy and his grandfather joyfully watch a gathering of butterflies in Mexico.

El camino de Amelia by Linda Jacobs Altman, illustrated by Enrique O. Sánchez, translated by Daniel Santacruz. Lee & Low Books, 1993.
This is the Spanish version of *Amelia's Road*.

Caribbean Dream written and illustrated by Rachel Isadora. Putnam, 1998.
This book portrays a lyrical and evocative dreamscape of the Caribbean.

Carlos, Light the Farolito by Jean Ciavonne, illustrated by Donna Clair. Clarion, 1995.
When his parents and grandfather are late on Christmas Eve, it's up to Carlos to take over his grandfather's role in Las Posadas.

A Day's Work by Eve Bunting, illustrated by Ronald Himler. Clarion Books, 1994.
When Francisco tries to help his grandfather find work, he discovers that though the old man cannot speak English, he has something even more valuable to teach Francisco.

The Desert Mermaid/La sirena del desierto by Alberto Blanco, illustrated by Patricia Revah, English translation by Barbara Paschke. Children's Book Press/Libros para niños, 1992.
A desert mermaid seeks to save her people by rediscovering songs of their ancestors.

From Here to There by Margery Cuyler, illustrated by Yu Cha Pak. Henry Holt & Company, 1999.
Maria introduces herself as a member of a family having a definite address and place.

The Garden of Happiness by Erika Tamar, illustrated by Barbara Lambase. Harcourt Brace, 1996.
Marisol and her neighbors turn a vacant New York City lot into a community garden.

Going Home *by Eve Bunting, illustrated by David Díaz. HarperCollins, 1996.*
Although a Mexican family comes to the United States to work as farm laborers so that their children will have opportunities, the parents still consider Mexico their home.

The Gullywasher written and illustrated by Joyce Rossi. Rising Moon Press, 1995.
Leticia's grandfather explains his wrinkles, white hair, round belly, and stooped frame.

How Nanita Learned to Make Flan by Campbell Geeslin, illustrated by Petra Mathers. Atheneum, 1999.
A Mexican cobbler is so busy that he cannot make shoes for his daughter, so she makes shoes, which take her to a rich man's home, where she must clean and cook all day.

Jalapeña Bagels by Natasha Wing, illustrated by Robert Casilla. Atheneum, 1996.
For International Day, Pablo wants something to reflect the cultures of both his parents.

Lights on the River by Jane Resh Thomas, illustrated by Michael Dooling. Hyperion, 1994.
Teresa, daughter of migrant workers, keeps memories alive in her heart.

Lupe & Me by Elizabeth Spurr, illustrated by Enrique O. Sánchez. Harcourt Brace & Co., 1995.
Seven-year-old Susan forms a special friendship with her family's young housekeeper, Lupe, who introduces her to Mexican customs and the Spanish language.

Manuela's Gift by Kristyn Rehling Estes, illustrated by Claire Cotts. Chronicle Books, 1999.
Manuela wants a dress for her birthday, but is disappointed when she receives a hand-me-down instead.

A Monster Is Hiding/El monstruo escondido written and illustrated by Bianca Cowan. O'Hollow, 1999.
This bilingual story tells about a child who is afraid of the monsters under the bed.

My Dog Is Lost by Ezra Jack Keats, illustrated by Pat Cherr. Viking, 1960, 1999.
Two days after arriving in New York from Puerto Rico, eight-year-old Juanito, who speaks no English, loses his dog and searches over the city, making friends along the way.

My Mexico/México mío: Poems by Tony Johnston, illustrated by F. John Sierra. Putnam's Sons, 1999.
These are poems about Mexico in English and Spanish.

My Two Worlds by Ginger Gordon, photographs by Martha Cooper. Clarion Books, 1993.
This book contrasts the worlds of a Dominican American girl who lives in New York City, speaks Spanish as her native language, and frequently returns to her island home.

Pumpkin Fiesta by Caryn Yacowitz, illustrated by Joe Cepeda. HarperCollins, 1998.
Hoping to win a prize for the best pumpkin, Fernando tries to copy Juana's gardening techniques, but without watching to see the effort and love she puts into her work.

El sancocho del sábado by Leyla Torres. Farrar Straus & Giroux, 1995.
This is the Spanish version of *Saturday Sancocho*.

Saturday Sancocho by Leyla Torres. Farrar Straus & Giroux, 1995.
Maria Lili and her grandmother barter a dozen eggs at the market square to get the ingredients to cook their traditional Saturday chicken sancocho.

Somos un arco by Nancy María Grande Tabor, edited by Elena Dworkin Wright. Charlesbridge Publishing, 1995.
This is the Spanish version of *We Are a Rainbow*.

Speak English for Us, Marisol! by Karen English, illustrated by Enrique O. Sánchez. Albert Whitman & Company, 2000.
Marisol, who is bilingual, is sometimes overwhelmed when her Spanish-speaking family members and neighbors need her to translate for them.

The Terrible Tragadabas/El terrible Tragadabas by Joe Hayes, illustrated by Lucy Jelinek. Trails West Pub., 1987.
Three sisters run away in fright from the terrible Tragadabas but in the end the Tragadabas gets a terrible shock of his own.

Tío Armando by Florence Parry Heide and Roxanne Heide Pierce, illustrated by Ann Grifalconi. Lothrop, Lee & Shepard, 1998.
Lucita's great-uncle Armando comes to live with them and teaches her truths about life.

Tonio's Cat by Mary Calhoun, illustrated by Edward Martínez. Morrow, 1996.
Toughy begins to fill the emptiness Tonio feels because he had to leave his dog.

Under the Lemon Moon by Edith Hope Fine, illustrated by René King Moreno. Lee & Low Books, 1999.
The theft of lemons from her tree leads Rosalinda to an encounter with the Old One and to an understanding of generosity and forgiveness.

Vroomaloom Zoom by John Coy, illustrated by Joe Cepeda. Crown Publishers, 2000.
Daddy takes Carmela on an imaginary car ride, lulling her to sleep with various sounds.

We Are a Rainbow written and illustrated by Nancy María Grande Tabor. Charlesbridge Publishing, 1997.
Simple text and illustrations explore similarities and differences that a child recognizes after moving to the United States from a Spanish-speaking country.

Index